MAKE YOUR OWN CLASSICAL GUITAR

MAKE YOUR OWN
Classical Guitar

STANLEY DOUBTFIRE

LONDON
VICTOR GOLLANCZ LTD
1981

ISBN 0 575 02980 3

To my wife Dianne
with all my love and thanks

Designed by
Leslie and Lorraine Gerry

Filmset and printed in Great Britain by
BAS Printers Limited,
Over Wallop, Hampshire

CONTENTS

'If any man love the labour of any trade . . .
the gods have called him.'

Robert Louis Stevenson

INTRODUCTION

The beauty of the classical guitar is attracting world-wide appreciation as more and more people are learning to play, but how many of us could justify the outlay of hundreds of pounds to purchase a first class instrument? Cheap guitars are difficult to play and not very beautiful, so another way has to be found if we wish to acquire a good one. My way (and I hope yours, too) is to make my own. Not only will you possess a fine guitar at a fraction of the cost of a top quality professionally-made one, but it will be your individual creation.

If you have never handled a chisel or plane, then perhaps guitar-making is not for you, but anyone used to working with wood or who has model-making experience should have the necessary skills. Great care and patience are needed, of course, but you will be carried along by your own enthusiasm and the pleasure of seeing the instrument gradually taking shape.

The classical guitar, as played by great masters such as Andrés Segovia, Julian Bream and John Williams, has been likened to a full orchestra in miniature. In such hands it reaches the peak of artistic expression, but an amateur can find great joy in playing a good guitar, especially one of his own making. If you follow carefully the step-by-step instructions set out in this book, you will one day be the possessor of an instrument with good looks and a beautiful tone.

PART 1

1 GOOD VIBRATIONS

Before considering the materials used in construction, it is helpful to have an understanding of the way in which the sound is produced. Nearly all stringed instruments are the same in this respect; the difference between them is in the method used to set the strings in motion.

Plucking a guitar string starts the vibrations which are transmitted by the bridge to the body. These responses ripple across the sound-board in concentric circles and are supplemented by the vibrations of the sides and back. The air inside the body of the instrument begins to respond in sympathy and the resulting pulses, or sound waves, are ejected through the sound-hole. The slightly domed back of the guitar, rather like a concave mirror on the inside, acts as a reflector.

The quality of the sound depends upon many related factors; the most important of these is the wood chosen for the sound-board. Other important considerations are the body size and shape, the thicknesses of the sound-board, back and sides, wood grain configurations, and interior strutting. An ideal situation would be one in which all the various components integrate so perfectly with one another that every note from the lowest 'E' to the highest 'B' has a clear singing tone. Unfortunately, this happy state of affairs is rarely achieved; in fact, it is probably true to say that the perfect guitar has yet to be made. But the possibility is there, and I can well remember the excitement of stringing up my first instrument and plucking the strings!

Tonal balance is perhaps the most elusive quality. Every note in a chord should have the same duration of sound, so that we are not left with one or two notes singing on after the rest have died. Another distinguishing feature of the top quality classical guitar is the evenness of tone from bass to treble, and it seems to be entirely dependent upon the quality of the sound-board. Time and patience spent on this component will be well repaid. It has to be thin so that it can vibrate freely but it must also be strong enough to stand up to the tension of the strings. Strength is achieved by a pattern of strutting glued underneath but unless this system is carefully designed it can have a dampening effect on the sound. A good strutting arrangement spreads the vibrations across the whole sound-board and improves sound-production enormously. A great variety of bracing systems has been devised, the pros and cons causing a lot of controversy amongst guitarists and makers. Antonio Torres (1817–1892), the originator of the modern guitar, started it all with his famous fan-strutting design (1.1), and it is still used today. Strutting had been in use for many years before Torres' time, and is found in guitars made in the eighteenth century by Pagés and Panormo, but Torres co-ordinated all the ideas of the past, using the best of them in his own instruments. In their search for the best possible sound, many modern makers design their own systems, but these are almost invariably based on the Torres pattern.

This great Spanish luthier also standardised the length of the strings at 65cm. Commonly called the 'scale-length', this measurement is nowadays considered to be a little short. A longer string allows a larger body and this produces a bigger sound for today's concert performances. There is a limit, however, to the overall size increase, not only because the distance between frets becomes greater and makes the instrument more difficult to play, but also because the larger sound-board needs stronger bracing, and this has the effect of deadening its responses. Some of the best makers of the present day still use the 65cm scale-length, insisting that there are other factors in the construction which give their guitars a 'big' sound. So there is still plenty of scope for improvement by those of an experimental disposition.

The development of the classical guitar over four centuries has produced an instrument of increased size and refined shape (1.2), but the constant obsession of the maker is to increase the volume of sound and improve the tonal quality. The area where most of these improvements have taken place is in the sound-board and strutting system, and new ideas are constantly being born, pushing the development of the instrument still further.

The right materials are vital to the construction of a good musical instrument, but almost equally important is the environment in which it is built. Humidity fluctuations play havoc with wood, and the most damaging change is from a damp atmosphere to a dry one; the sound-boards and backs of guitars split as they dry out. The best way to avoid these catastrophes is to start with well seasoned, dry timber, and then to build the instrument in a dry atmosphere. Such a guitar will

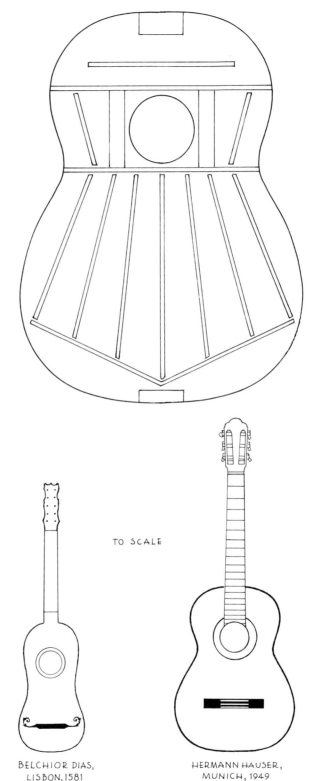

1.1 **Traditional sound-board strutting system**

TO SCALE

BELCHIOR DIAS, LISBON, 1581

HERMANN HAUSER, MUNICH, 1949

1.2 **Nearly four centuries of development**

swell slightly if exposed to damper conditions, but will be unlikely to split as it dries out again, unless of course, the changes are very severe.

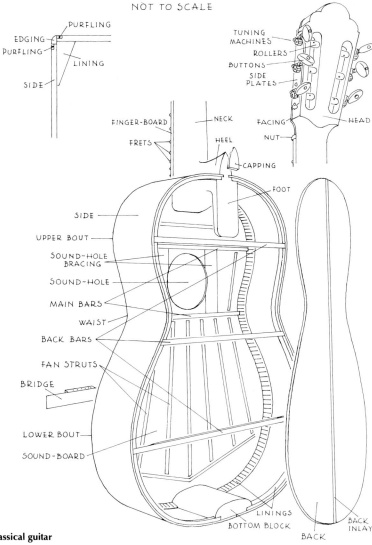

NOT TO SCALE

PURFLING
EDGING
PURFLING
SIDE
LINING

TUNING MACHINES
ROLLERS
BUTTONS
SIDE PLATES
FACING
NUT
HEAD

FINGER-BOARD
NECK
FRETS
HEEL
CAPPING
FOOT

SIDE
UPPER BOUT
SOUND-HOLE BRACING
SOUND-HOLE
MAIN BARS
WAIST
BACK BARS
FAN STRUTS
BRIDGE
LOWER BOUT
SOUND-BOARD
LININGS
BOTTOM BLOCK
BACK INLAY
BACK

2.1 **The parts of a classical guitar**

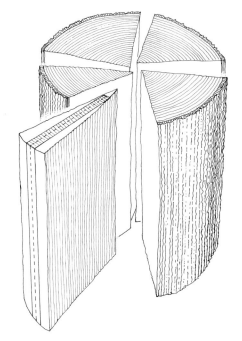

2.2 **Section of a spruce tree**

2   MATERIALS

The first thing that strikes you when you see a good classical guitar is the beauty of the wood. Several kinds of timber are used to construct one guitar, each performing its individual task. Very good instruments have been made from a wide variety of woods, but traditionally, the woods chosen for their tonal qualities as well as for their grain and colour, are spruce, maple, mahogany, rosewood, ebony, cedar and willow.

The body of a guitar is made from timber which has been cut in a special way (2·2). The log is cleft into segments which are then sawn radially so that the annual rings cross at right angles to the faces of the boards.

Spruce is the only wood really suitable for the sound-board. The best variety is known by many names, some of them quite misleading such as Swiss Pine, White Pine, Norway Spruce, etc., but in fact, it is the common or garden Christmas Tree, and the botanical name of the species is *Picea excelsa*. A native of northern Europe, it can be found on most mountain ranges from the Pyrenees to a latitude of about 68°N. It is a strikingly beautiful tree, and has been used as an ornamental feature in English gardens since about 1600. It frequently grows to a height of 50 metres and has wide-spreading branches, the lowest and longest of these often drooping to touch the ground. The foliage is dense and dark green, with cylindrical cones 10–20cm long at the ends of the upper branches. The straight, tapering trunk sometimes has a diameter of 2 metres at its base, and the trees are often hundreds of years old.

The finest sound-board timber, grown specially for the purpose, comes from high on the mountain-side near the timber-line where the trees are very slow-growing. The cold environment produces closely spaced annual rings, and the best quality boards have a grain-spacing of less than 1mm, with the lines running perfectly straight from top to bottom. A gradual widening of the spacing across the board is perfectly acceptable, but it must not be too exaggerated. Spruce of this quality is unsurpassed, and has been used since ancient times for the sound-boards of the finest musical instruments. It has a high sensitivity to vibrations so that it resonates with a clear note when struck, and possesses a fair amount of strength combined with elasticity. Unfortunately, the highest quality tone-wood is becoming scarce and very expensive, causing makers to look elsewhere for their sound-boards. Carefully selected cedar is the best alternative and some well-known luthiers are beginning to use it, but it will always be inferior to the finest *Picea excelsa*.

Sound-boards are made from a plank sawn open like the pages of a book (2.3). These two matching rough-sawn planks are about 5mm thick and must be glued edge to edge (jointed), before being planed and smoothed down to the finished thickness of 2–2½mm. This butt joint falls exactly on the centre-line of the guitar and ensures that the grain is symmetrical in both halves of the sound-board.

Backs and sides (the sides are sometimes called ribs), are purchased in matched sets so that the grain-pattern and colour will be uniform. Rosewood is favoured by most makers because the dark, rich colour contrasts so well with the spruce sound-board (2.4). Two main varieties are suitable for guitar making: Brazilian, known in the trade as Rio rosewood because it comes from the provinces of Rio de Janeiro and Bahia (the Brazilians call it *jacaranda*), and Indian (Bombay) rosewood. Rio rosewood is very scarce, and large pieces of the necessary high quality are extremely expensive and almost impossible to find. Bombay rosewood, fortunately, is in fairly plentiful supply and more reasonably priced. Darker in colour than the Rio variety, it is beautifully marked with brown, black and mauve streaks. The trees are very large, but they decay in the centre before reaching maturity, so they are usually hollow inside. This means that quarter-sawn pieces wider than about 30cm are unobtainable. Rosewood is very resinous, and with its unpredictable grain directions, can be difficult to work.

Maple is equally good tonally for the backs and sides. The best varieties for our purpose being commonly known as the European or Great Maple (botanical name, *Acer pseudoplatanus*), known in England as sycamore, and the common maple (*Acer campestre*). This highly prized timber is heavy, hard and strong, and has differing grain characteristics. The richly flamed pieces, although extremely beautiful, are very difficult to work due to their complex grain structure, but straighter-grained pieces are fairly easily obtainable. After varnishing, the wood matures to a glowing, golden colour.

Backs, like sound-boards, are 'book-matched' and have to be jointed. The sides are bent to shape on a

2.3 **The two matching boards before jointing**

2.4 **Rosewood for the back**

bending-iron after being reduced to the correct thickness by planing and scraping.

The neck is usually made from the finest straight-grained mahogany, or Honduras cedar, although maple

2.5 The raw materials unpacked

mountainside, select the tree he wants, then have it felled, sawn up and transported to his timber store! This, of course, is pure fantasy for most of us, and all the materials we require must be purchased from a specialist supplier, including the strips of willow for the linings, spruce for the strutting and bottom block, edgings and decorative purfling strips, rosettes for the coloured inlay around the sound-hole, fret-wire and tuning-machines (2.5).

Choose a supplier from the list at the end of this chapter, and send for his catalogue. There are varying qualities of wood to choose from, and my advice would be to buy the best if you have had some experience in precision carpentry and the making of other types of musical instruments. Otherwise, purchase second quality materials for your first guitar. You can then work through all the procedures without the worry of spoiling a rare and valuable piece of wood. Later, for your Mark 2, only the best will do! Inspect all materials carefully on arrival and return immediately any item that is unsatisfactory.

is sometimes used, and the figuring can be very attractive, especially when tastefully matched with maple back and sides. Many varieties of mahogany come from central America and the West Indies, the finest being known as Honduras mahogany (*Swietenia macrophylla*). It is a large tree with compound leaves rather like an ash, and is reputed to have been discovered by the carpenter on Sir Walter Raleigh's ship in 1595. Other sources of this valuable timber are India and South Africa. West African mahogany is softer, with a coarser grain, but it is lighter in weight than Honduras. The best quality Honduras mahogany has a fine, hard texture, and a rich, reddish-brown colour. Some of the best craftsmen in the world have used it for the construction of their exquisite furniture.

Finger-boards on the finest guitars are made from ebony, and it contrasts perfectly with the metal frets. Rosewood is often used but it is not as hard wearing. The best ebony (*Diospyros ebenum*), comes from India and Ceylon. The heart-wood only is used. It is very heavy, deep black in colour, and although very hard, it has an even texture. Ebony has been held in the highest esteem by craftsmen since biblical times.

Bridges can be made from either ebony or rosewood, but quarter-sawn rosewood is the traditional material. Ivory is best for the saddle and nut, but it is not easy to find nowadays so bone is sometimes used instead. It is a poor substitute because it discolours fairly quickly. Second-hand shops are the guitar maker's ivory hunting ground.

The luthier's dream is to travel to a timber forest on a

WOOD AND ACCESSORIES REQUIRED

Sound-board:
European spruce (*Picea excelsa*).
Two pieces, radially sawn and book-matched, 51cm × 20cm × 4mm minimum.

Back and Sides:
Rosewood or maple in a book-matched set.
Back: 51cm × 20cm × 4mm (two pieces).
Sides: 81cm × 10cm × 4mm (two pieces).

Neck:
Honduras mahogany, Honduras cedar, or maple, straight-grained.
107cm × 7·5cm × 23.5mm.

Finger-board:
Ebony or rosewood, 46cm × 7cm × 8mm.

Bridge:
Rosewood or ebony, 20cm × 3·5cm × 12mm.

Linings:
Four willow strips, 75cm × 1·5cm × 5mm.

Front strutting:
Spruce strips, preferably cleft, sometimes sold in rough-sawn sets, otherwise, sizes as in Chapter 16.

Back strutting:
Three pieces of spruce or maple for a maple guitar, mahogany for a rosewood guitar.

Bottom Block:
Spruce, 10cm × 6·5cm × 17mm.

Edging:
Rosewood, ebony or a light coloured hardwood.

Purfling:
For a maple guitar, ten strips, black/white/black.
For a rosewood guitar, two strips, black/white/black,
eight strips, white/black/white.

Rosette:
Large selection to choose from—send to suppliers for
their coloured sample-card. Alternatively, you may
wish to make a rosette to your own design. A brief
description will be found in Chapter 15, but fully
detailed instructions are given in *The Classical Guitar*
by McLeod and Welford, The Dryad Press.

Frets:
Nickel silver fret-wire with studded tang, 122cm.

Tuning Machines:
Precision made, with large diameter rollers for nylon
strings.

Ivory:
Two pieces for the Bridge Saddle and Nut.
Two pieces for the Bridge Tie-Block edging.

SUPPLIERS (U.K.)

Sydney Evans, Ltd. (All types and grades of wood and
accessories).
The Violin Shop, 45, Regent Place, Birmingham,
B1 3NB. Tel: 233 1741

Henry Flack, Ltd. (Finishing materials).
Borough Works, Croydon Road, Elmers End,
Beckenham, Kent.

F. T. Morell & Co. (Finishing materials).
330, Old Street, London, EC1 V9DP

The World of Wood (All materials and large selection
of veneers).
Industrial Estate, Mildenhall, Suffolk, IP28 7AY

All the above suppliers are included in a booklet
entitled *Directory of Suppliers to Craftsmen Musical
Instrument Makers* by Ian Firth, available from Crafts
Council, 12, Waterloo Place, London SW1Y 4AU.

SUPPLIERS (U.S.A. AND CANADA)

H. Behlen & Bro. Inc.
Box 698, New York, N.Y.

Albert Constantine & Son, Inc.
2050, Eastchester Road, Bronx, N.Y. 10461

Ibex Company
Millerton, New York, N.Y.

Bill Lewis Music Ltd.
3607, West Broadway, Vancouver 8, B.C., Canada

Marina Music
1892, Union Street, San Francisco, California

Metropolitan Music Co.
222, Park Avenue South, New York, N.Y.

Sherry-Brener, Ltd.
3145, W. 63rd Street, Chicago, Illinois

Vitali Import Co.
5944–48, Atlantic Blvd., Maywood, California

J. F. Wallo
1319, 'F' Street N.W., Washington, D.C.

H. L. Wild, Co.
510, East Eleventh Street, New York, N.Y.

3 TOOLS

3.1 **Some important tools.**
1 **Cabinet scraper;** 2 **Backsaw;**
3 **Stanley knife;** 4 **Caliper;**
5 **30mm Gouge;** 6 **10mm**
Gouge; 7 **Dividers;** 8 **Purfling**
cutter; 9 **Sanding block;**
10 **Fret-wire clippers;** 11
Spokeshave; 12 **11mm Bit;**
13 **16mm Bit;** 14 **5mm Chisel;**
15 **25mm Chisel;** 16 **10mm Chisel;**
17 **Block plane;** 18 **Circle cutter**

outside building. When I used to work in an out-building away from the house, I kept everything indoors, only taking to the workshop the part I was working on at the time. Try not to be put off by adverse working conditions; some of the world's finest craftsmanship has been accomplished in situations which were far from ideal.

A movable light source of the Anglepoise type is very useful, because you often need to shine a light on to exactly the right spot when shaping the Head, or cutting the Purfling grooves.

PLANES

We've all heard the bad workman blaming his tools, but the good workman is severely handicapped with poor tools. Nothing is more frustrating than attempting to smooth a beautiful piece of wood with a blunt plane. We've all done it at times when we've felt tired and just couldn't be bothered to take out the plane-iron and sharpen it yet again. But my advice would be to stop work for a while, do something else, then come back to the bench refreshed and determined to make that plane cut like a razor!

You will need three types of plane for guitar making, all preferably made of steel because these are the easiest to adjust.

The Fore Plane is more versatile than the Jointer and longer than the Jack. It is used for flattening the large surfaces of the Sound-board, Back and Sides, and for joining the matched halves of the Sound-board and Back. It should be at least 50cm long to produce the perfectly true edges for this joint (3.2). The fore plane can also be used in the thicknessing operation to be described in a later chapter.

The most important possession of an instrument-maker is his workbench. Ideally, it should be rock steady, level, and with a perfectly flat work-top. My bench is far from level, and it is so old that its top is gouged and scored by many decades of hard labour. Nevertheless, I love it. I get over the unevenness of its surface by clamping a large piece of block-board to its top. So don't worry if you haven't got a fine carpenter's bench with a fixed vice, because a strong table and a clamp-on vice will serve almost as well. Try to find some means of anchoring it to the floor or to a wall; metal angle brackets might solve the problem. José Romanillos, now an internationally famous luthier, built his first guitar on the kitchen table, so you don't need a lot of space. A bench at the end of the garage could be your answer, but dampness is a problem with an unheated

BOARD

SHORT PLANE RIDES THE BUMPS

BOARD

LONG PLANE REMOVES THE BUMPS

3.2 **Long and short planes**

The Smoothing Plane is about 24cm long. It is used to obtain that satin smooth finish which we all admire so much, and it must be capable of removing the very finest shavings.

The Block Plane is a very small plane that fits into the palm of your hand, and it is used for trimming, cleaning up edges, and shaping.

SHARPENING

When you buy a new plane it can't be put into use straight from the shop; its cutting edge has to be trued up and sharpened. As this operation has to be performed at frequent intervals throughout the life of the tool, it might be helpful to describe the process in some detail. First of all, the cutting blade, or plane-iron has to be removed. This is usually held in place by a simple clamping device. Then, after loosening a large screw, the iron can be separated from the cap. The cutting edge should first be ground back on a carborundum wheel (being careful not to overheat the iron) to an angle of 25 degrees. Then the keen edge is set at an angle of 30 degrees on a fine carborundum or India oil stone. It is very important that your sharpening stone is flat. If yours is old and worn, you must either have it flattened or buy a new one.

The art of sharpening can be learnt very quickly with a little practice, and it's well worth the trouble. The main difficulty lies in keeping the correct angle on the cutting edge, and the secret is to rub with long, slow, even strokes on a perfectly flat oil stone, inspecting the edge at every third or fourth stroke. When a burr appears on the flat side of the iron, rub on this side, but holding it flat down on the stone. *Never* put an angle on the flat side. Continue rubbing like this on both sides alternately until the burr just begins to peel off, and then finish the edge on a piece of leather or fine cloth. If you have produced a good edge, you should be able to shave the hairs on the back of your wrist, cleanly, like a razor. Take care, though, these edges are dangerous!

Put the plane together again very carefully, to avoid damaging the edge, screwing on the cap so that about 1mm of the flat side of the cutting edge is visible. Set up the blade by sighting along the sole from the front, adjusting the controls provided until you can just see an even strip of cutting edge beginning to appear through the slot. Test and finally adjust for depth of cut on a clean piece of softwood.

CHISELS

Bevel-edge chisels are the most useful. These have cut-away sides, making them easier to use in confined spaces. Three sizes are sufficient—25mm, 10mm and 5mm.

Firmer-gouges are required for shaping the Heel—a large one, 30mm, for roughing out, and a 10mm size for finer work.

If you can sharpen a plane iron, you will find no difficulty with a chisel. The angles are the same: grind back to 25 degrees, and sharpen at 30 degrees. Firmer-gouges are ground and sharpened on the outside curve, and an even, rocking motion is used as you rub. The inner curve is left untouched except for removing the burr with a small piece of stone shaped to a curve on a grinding wheel; a broken piece from an old oil stone would serve very well.

SPOKESHAVE

This is a handy tool for shaping the Neck, but a little practice is required if you are not used to handling one. The cutting blade is ground and sharpened like a plane-iron.

CABINET SCRAPER

This is a traditional tool of the master-craftsman. In skilled hands it can produce a smoothness of surface which is unobtainable with the finest sandpaper. It can be purchased in most tool shops and its simplicity is a delight in this sophisticated age. It consists of a piece of steel 12·5cm × 6cm × 1mm thick, which you must prepare in such a way that a burr is created on its edges, and it is this burr which does the smoothing. To set up a cabinet scraper you must first true up both the long edges on an oil stone. A squared up block of wood held on the stone will act as a guide while rubbing the edges, and ensure that they are square and sharp (3.3 and 3.4)

3.3 **Squaring up the edge**

3.4 Flattening the side

3.5 Creating a burr

3.6 Turning over the burr

3.7 The scraper in use

A round piece of steel (the back of a gouge, for instance), is then rubbed along both sides of the squared edges, but held at a slight angle to the surface—a few degrees is sufficient (3.5).

The final operation, rubbing the steel along the four edges, turns the burr over to form the cutting edge (3.6).

In use, the scraper is held in both hands and pushed away from you by the thumbs. The correct angle to the work must be adjusted by experiment, but it is roughly 45 degrees, pointing away from you (3.7). The four edges are brought into use in turn, before the sharpening operation has to be repeated.

SURFORM (flat blade)
SURFORM (round blade)
These tools have replaceable blades, and are useful for rough shaping. They cut very fast, and you can easily remove too much wood if you are not extremely careful.

FILES
Large, flat (medium cut).
Small, flat (fine cut).
Large, round (medium cut).
Small, round (fine cut).
Set of needle files.

*SANDING BLOCK
Cork is best, but a squared up block of softwood serves well.

*SANDING STICKS
Flat (coarse grain).
Flat (fine grain).
Round (coarse grain).
Round (fine grain).
It is well worth the time to make these simple tools; they are in constant use.

SAWS
Panel.
Large tenon.
Small tenon.
Frame-saw or coping-saw.
Small backsaw with very fine cut.
Fret-saw.
Small hacksaw.

DRILLS
Carpenter's brace with Jennings pattern bits, sizes 16mm and 11mm.
Wheelbrace with a set of twist drills.
A vertical, bench drilling machine is an advantage if you

already have one.

HAMMER
Light-weight for fretting.

WOODEN MALLET

SCREWDRIVERS
Large.
Small (electrician's).

STANLEY KNIFE
With spare blades.

WIRE CLIPPERS
For fretting.

PENCIL COMPASS

STEEL DIVIDERS

CARPENTER'S SQUARE

SLIDING BEVEL

STEEL STRAIGHT-EDGE

STEEL MEASURING TAPE

MARKING GAUGE

CARPENTER'S BENCH-VICE
The jaws must be protected with pieces of soft-wood to avoid bruising the work.

PORTABLE VICE
This clamps to the work-top where you want it.

CRAMPS
Two (or more) large 'G' cramps.
Four (or more) small 'G' cramps.

Many of the tools listed above can be found in the average handyman's tool kit, but the following items are peculiar to guitar making.

*GUITAR-MAKER'S CRAMPS
Three are required. These are invaluable for light cramping and holding jobs, strutting the Sound-board, and gluing on the Bridge.

*THICKNESSING CALIPER
If guitar-making is going to be a serious activity, you will certainly want to make more than one, so it would be worth buying a special caliper gauge with a clock dial which measures thicknesses down to one-tenth of a millimetre. Otherwise, a useful pencil caliper can be made very simply.

PURFLING CUTTER
This is needed for Edgings, and inlaying the decorative strips. They can be purchased from musical instrument makers' suppliers (see page 13), and are usually made of brass. Home-made wooden ones tend to become inaccurate after a lot of use.

*CIRCLE CUTTER
This implement is essential for inlaying the Rosette and for cutting out the Sound-hole. It is difficult to find a ready-made one of sufficient accuracy for this work, so you will find instructions for making your own in Chapter 4.

*BENDING IRON
The Sides of a guitar are bent on a hot iron. This can be a specially made electric iron with a thermostatically controlled element, obtainable from one of the suppliers listed. You can, alternatively, make you own, using an electric soldering iron and a piece of copper pipe.

*See Chapter 4, TOOLS YOU CAN MAKE.

4   TOOLS YOU CAN MAKE

SANDING-BLOCKS

A piece of softwood (knot-free deal or pine), 7·5cm × 4·5cm × 2cm, is all that is required for a general-duty block. Square it up, and wrap a strip of medium grade sand-paper around it, fastened along one edge with drawing-pins. You can then renew the sand-paper easily when it wears out. Several blocks can be made of various sizes and grades of sand-paper.

SANDING-STICKS (4.1)

These are worth their weight in gold to the guitar maker. Flat sanding-sticks are made from straight battens of knot-free timber (Parana pine, for example), 50cm × 4cm × 1·5cm. Aluminium Oxide abrasive paper has a longer life than sand-paper, and if you glue it on with a contact adhesive such as Evo-Stik, you will have a perfectly flat sanding surface which is renewable. Two sticks are sufficient—a coarse and a fine.

Round-sectioned sticks are made from two 30cm pieces of 15mm diameter dowel. The Aluminium Oxide paper is first cut to size. This can be done accurately in the following way: draw a pencil line straight down the length of the dowel and roll it over the paper, marking where the line starts and finishes. Cut the piece out with old scissors, and apply contact adhesive to dowel and paper. Wait for fifteen minutes or so, then roll it on.

GUITAR-MAKER'S CRAMP (4.2)

This wooden cramp can be purchased from specialist suppliers, but you can make three or four for the price of one. It has a deep throat to span the wide front of a guitar when gluing on the Strutting, and the lower section can be passed through the Sound-hole when gluing on the Bridge. It has a light, but firm gripping action, and the protected jaws won't damage the work. The quick-release lever works on the cam principle.

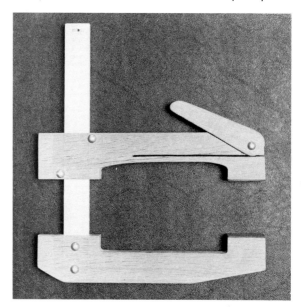

4.2 **Guitar maker's cramp**

4.1 **Coarse and fine sanding sticks**

Materials to make three cramps.

6 pieces of hardwood (preferably beech), 23cm × 4·5cm × 2cm.

3 pieces of hardwood (preferably beech), 10cm × 2·5cm × 2cm.

3 lengths of aluminium strip, 25cm × 2·5cm × 6mm.

15 aluminium rivets.

1 split pin.

3 pieces of old car tyre inner-tube (easily obtainable from a garage).

You will find it quicker to make all three at the same time.

Instructions

1   Cut out the shapes of the arms from the measurements on the drawing (4.3), and plane and sand them smooth.

2   Mark the position and size of the mortices directly from the aluminium strip.

3   Use a drill to remove the waste wood from the mortices and clean up the holes with a chisel. The lower arms should be a tight fit on the aluminium, but the upper ones must slide freely without too much play. Keep testing the fit as you chisel out the mortices.

4   Drill a 3mm hole in the upper arms where the end of the slot will come. This is to prevent splitting when the lever forces open the slot. Cut the slot down to the hole with a tenon saw.

5   Cut out the three levers, and sand them smooth.

6   Carefully mark out the tenons on the upper arms using a very sharp pencil. The waste can be cut away with a tenon saw after wedging open the slot (4.4).

7   Cut the mortices in the levers so that they are a loose fit on the tenons, and drill the off-centre rivet holes where indicated on the drawing.

8   Put one of the levers in place on its tenon, so that it is

just bearing on the sprung part of the arm, and clamp the assembly in a vice. Now drill through the tenon using the holes in the cheeks of the lever as a guide for the drill.

9   Drill all rivet holes, saw the rivets to length so that about 3mm protrude, and burr over the ends with a hammer, resting the heads of the rivets on a solid surface. The rivets in the upper arm are for reinforcement at the bearing sides of the mortice.

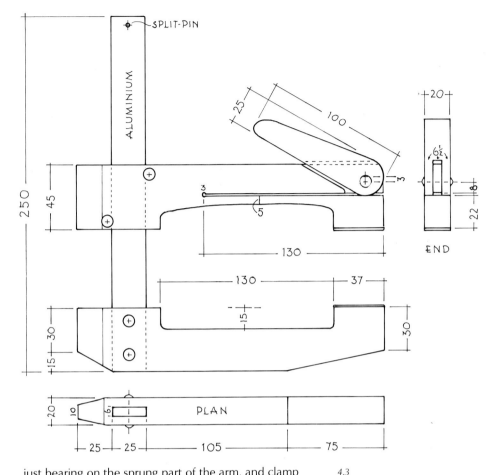

MEASUREMENTS IN MM?

4.3

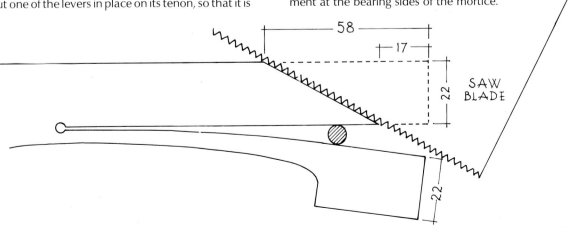

4.4 **Sawing the tenon**

19

10   Fit a split-pin at the top of each aluminium strip, and glue on the rubber jaw protectors with contact adhesive.

THICKNESSING CALIPER (4.5)

It is essential to have some way of testing the thicknesses of the Top, Back and Sides as you work. You can make this pencil caliper very easily. All you need is a length of hardwood, 25cm × 5·5cm × 20mm, cut out as shown in the diagram. The pencil should have a thick, soft lead (you can buy these in an artists'-materials shop). Machine-screws (obtainable from a hardware shop or garage), will cut their own threads in hardwood if you drill a slightly under-sized hole.

In use, the caliper is passed gently over the surface of the wood, and the pencil marks the areas to be removed. With practice, this tool can be almost as accurate as a clock caliper.

CIRCLE CUTTER (4.6)

Materials

1 piece of hardwood 15cm × 2cm × 1·5cm for the tool bar.
2 pieces of hardwood 6.5cm × 3cm × 1cm for the guide block cheeks.
1 piece of hardwood 6.5cm × 1.5cm × 1cm for the base.
One 5mm machine-screw with washer and nut.
One 8mm coach-bolt.
One small flat file for the cutter.
A small off-cut of laminated plastic (Formica) for the bearing surfaces.

Instructions

1   Cut out the cheeks and base of the guide block to the measurements shown, square them up, and glue them together with Cascamite (see GLUE, Chapter 5). Clamp in a vice until the glue has hardened, and then clean up with sandpaper.

4.5 Thicknessing caliper

MEASUREMENTS IN MMS

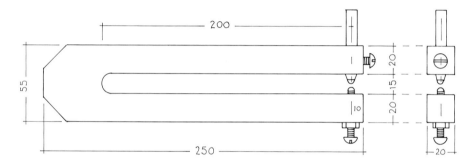

4.6 Circle cutter

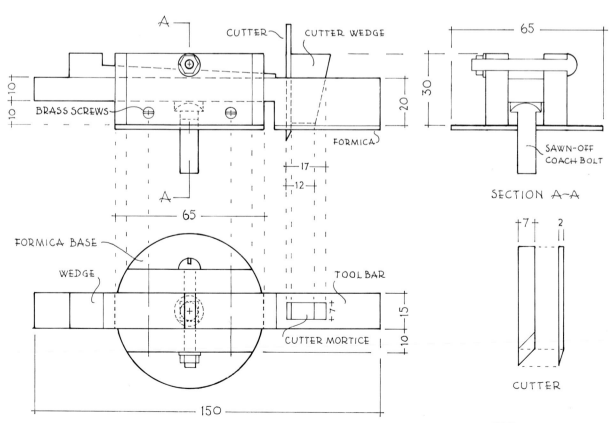

2   Cut out the tool bar slightly oversize. Save the waste piece for the wedge. Plane and sand the sides of the bar until it is a tight, sliding fit between the cheeks of the guide block. Face the bottom of the bar where shown with a piece of Formica glued on with contact adhesive.

3   Drill and chisel out the wedge-shaped mortice for the cutter, making sure that the perpendicular inside face is flat and perfectly square with the bottom of the tool bar.

4   Drill the cheeks of the guide block so that the machine-screw clears the top of the tool bar by about 3mm. Make the wedge.

5   Drill and counter-sink the base of the guide block so that the head of the coach-bolt will not turn. Saw off the bolt so that 2cm protrude below.

6   Cut a 65mm diameter circle of Formica, and drill the centre hole for the bolt. It is very important that there should be no play in this hole, or cutting accuracy will be impaired.

7   Make the cutter from a small file, by first grinding off the teeth. Grind the angle on the cutting end, and set back the edge like a chisel. Be very careful not to over-heat the file when grinding, or the hardness of the steel will be lost. Sharpen on an oilstone, keeping one face perfectly flat so that a perpendicular cut can be made.

8   Make the wedge to grip the cutter tightly in the mortice. Depth of cut is controlled by this wedging action.

9   Round the edges and corners of the Formica facing on the bottom of the tool bar, so that it will slide smoothly over the spruce sound-board without marking the delicate surface.

ELECTRIC BENDING IRON (4.7)
An electric soldering iron and an off-cut of copper pipe used in central-heating systems are the only require-ments. You will have to get the size of pipe that fits your particular soldering iron, but the 35mm size should be about right. It should be about 20cm long. Fix it tightly on to the iron by wedging large nails down the tube.

This bending iron can be gripped in a vice horizon-tally or vertically, by its handle.

VERY IMPORTANT: Make absolutely certain that your soldering iron is properly earthed, and that it is fitted with a three-pin, fused plug. If in doubt, have it checked by a qualified electrician.

WORK BOARD (4.8)
This guitar-shaped board can be clamped to the bench by its neck, allowing bindings to be wound right round it when gluing on the Back and Sound-board. Alter-natively, large rubber bands can be used to hold the guitar firmly while you are working on it. The hole enables you to pass a cramp up through the Sound-hole when gluing the Sound-board Strutting.

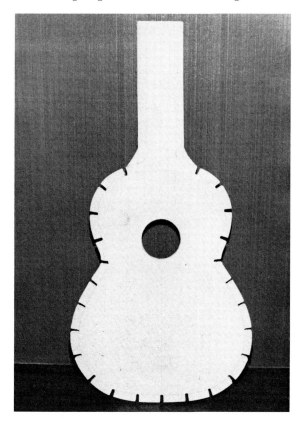

4.8 **Work board**

4.7 **Simple bending iron**

Rule a centre-line on to an 80cm × 45cm sheet of 25mm chipboard and draw round your template (Chapter 6). Draw the outline of the neck and then run a second line, 20mm outside the first one, around the complete shape. Cut out the board on this line with a frame-saw or coping-saw and clean up the edge. Drill the inner ends of the slots and saw out the waste. These slots are optional, but they allow the bindings or rubber bands to exert vertical pressure on the Sides when gluing on the Back and Sound-board. Cut out the 'sound-hole' with a coping-saw, or by drilling small holes around the circumference. Smooth the edges with a round surform and sanding stick.

HEAD DRILLING GUIDE

The string-slots in the Head are made by drilling 16mm holes at both ends of each slot, and sawing out the waste in between. These holes must be drilled at an exact right-angle to the face of the Head, and this is very difficult to achieve by eye alone. You cannot drill in from each side and hope to meet in the middle, because the veneer facing on the Head would be churned up by drilling in from the front. All the holes must be drilled straight through from the back (see Chapter 10). Accuracy can be assured by using a simple guide for the drill-bit. A block of hardwood (beech or oak) 10cm × 5·5cm × 10cm is all that is required.

Instructions

1   Square up the block accurately and mark the position of the guide-hole on the top and bottom faces with a marking gauge. All measurements are given on the drawing (4.9).

2   Clamp the block to a level surface and drill through half-way with a 16mm bit. Sight from all angles to keep the bit upright.

3   Turn the block over and drill through from the other side. If your drilling has gone well, the holes will meet in the middle of the block. (If not, you have another chance at the other end of your block.)

4   Plane the bottom face of the block (the face that will be clamped to the Head of the guitar) exactly square with the hole. This truing-up is easily tested by inserting a straight piece of wood (16mm dowel would be ideal) so that it projects from the hole. Check the squareness of the block face from both directions with a set-square laid against the dowel.

5   Mark the squared-up face very clearly for identification.

BACK BAR CLAMPING BATTENS

Three pieces of knot-free softwood can be used, and they should be at least 3cm × 2cm × 43cm long. Mark them out as in the diagram (4.10), drawing the curves with a flexible steel rule or a springy batten. Number them clearly. The hollows are scooped out with a spoke-shave and smoothed with a sanding stick. Test the accuracy of the curves with the springy batten, holding them up against the light. Remove any bumps with the round sanding stick.

BRIDGE CLAMPING BLOCK (Do not make this until the Sound-board has been completed, see Chapter 16). Square up a piece of knot free soft-wood 25cm × 4·5cm × 2cm. Arch one face so that it will fit exactly into the concave under-surface of the Sound-board. (This can be done with the help of the No. 3 Back bar clamping batten).

The grooves are cut to clear all the fan struts (and the Bridge Bar if you are incorporating one (4.11). Mark the positions of all the struts and cut the grooves to clear them by about one millimetre all round. The sides of the

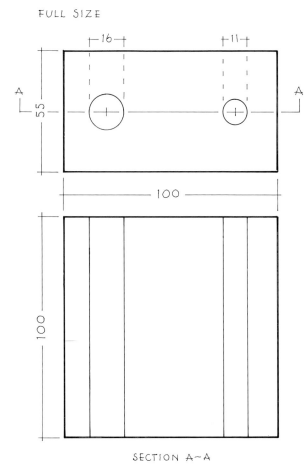

FULL SIZE

SECTION A—A

4.9 Head drilling guide

MEASUREMENTS IN MMS

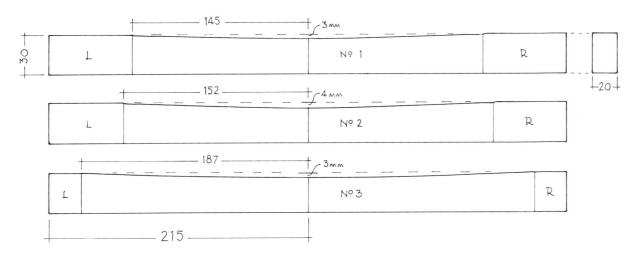

- 145 — 3mm

30 | L | No 1 | R

20

- 152 — 4mm

L | No 2 | R

- 187 — 3mm

L | No 3 | R

- 215 —

grooves are sawn down to the correct depth, then the waste is removed with a narrow chisel. Test the fit, clearing more wood from the grooves as necessary until the block rests on the Sound-board.

In use, the block is passed through the Sound-hole into the sound-chamber, where it is wedged up underneath the Sound-board whilst gluing on the Bridge.

INLAY STRIP THINNING TOOL

All that is required to make this useful little device is an off-cut of mahogany, 6cm × 1·5cm × 1cm to make a bridging block, and two strips of soft metal such as zinc, aluminium, tin-plate or brass, 6cm × 2cm × 0·5mm thick. The only important measurement is the thickness of the metal because this gauges the finished thickness of the inlay.

Cut out the clearance notch in the bridging block with a chisel, and clamp it over the ends of the metal strips on the edge of a board, as in the illustration (4.12).

Your inlay strip (cut from the edge of a sheet of veneer with a knife and metal straight-edge), is passed under the bridge, a cabinet scraper is pressed lightly down onto it, and the strip is pulled through. Repeat as necessary until the strip slides easily under the scraper. The tool can be seen in operation in Chapter 20, Figure 20.15.

A variety of inlay thicknesses can be produced by simply substituting different sizes of metal strips, or by doubling them up.

4.12 **Inlay strip thinning tool**

5   GLUE

There are many different types of glue available today for every conceivable fixing job, but some of these formulations are quite unsuitable for guitar making. There are four glues, however, which have been found to be the best for our special needs. The one to use for a particular job will be given in the appropriate chapter. Purists will raise their hands in horror at my inclusion of the modern 'concoctions', but it is my belief that their use does not affect the tone of an instrument, and that many beautiful examples of the luthier's art would still exist today had resin glues been available to the old instrument-makers.

ANIMAL GLUE
This is the traditional glue of the violin maker. It is made from the hooves, hides, bones and sinews of animals, and it is purchased in thin sheets or pellets. It has to be melted down by the user in a special glue pot with an external water container, and used whilst hot. The chief argument put forward in its favour is that, in the event of an internal repair being needed, the Sound-board or Back can be removed with a knife dipped in hot water to melt the glue. This may be an invaluable attribute where violins are concerned, but in the case of the guitar it is extremely doubtful. For instance, before ungluing the Sound-board, the Edgings, Purflings and Finger-board would have to be removed, and this could be a very destructive operation. Removal of the Back would present additional problems due to the three Back Bars jointed into the Linings. In any case, unlike the violin, most internal repair jobs on a guitar can be carried out through the Sound-hole.

Animal glue is very strong if correctly prepared and used fresh, but it has been discovered that glue failure can occur because the mixture is not moisture-proof, and bacteria can live in the glued joint, slowly breaking it down.

UREA FORMALDEHYDE (Cascamite One Shot)
This is a modern resin glue. It is purchased as a powder which you mix with cold water, and it contains its own hardener. This glue sets by chemical action, and is extremely strong and waterpoof. To prepare it, follow the manufacturer's instructions, but for maximum strength, don't make it too thin. The consistency of full cream is about right. Mix only the quantity you think you'll need for a particular job; if there is some left over, it will have to be thrown away because the setting action starts to work as soon as you add the water.

EPOXY (Araldite)
This is one of the strongest adhesives available. It is even used in the assembly of metal masts for yachts! Two separate tubes are provided, one of base, and one of hardener. You have to mix an equal quantity of each part. Again, setting is by chemical action, resulting in a waterproof joint of unbelievable strength. I glued the broken handles on two coffee mugs six years ago, and they are still in every-day use, but there are only one or two instances in guitar making where such a bond is necessary.

P.V.A. (Polyvinylacetate)
(Evo-Stik Resin W.)
This is another modern adhesive which would undoubtedly have been put to good use by Stradivari and his colleagues. It is a resin based, ready-mixed white emulsion in a plastic container with a spout. The bonding strength is not quite as good as Cascamite, but its convenience makes it ideal for many jobs in guitar making. It is fairly waterproof, and it lasts for years in its container if you push a screw into the hole in the spout after use. Some other makes of P.V.A., or 'white glue' are unsuitable because they do not dry hard and transparent, and a joint under stress is liable to 'creep.' This glue is not recommended for gluing on the Bridge.

true rectangle, then rule the grid-lines with a try-square 1cm apart, using the straightest edge of the board as your centre line. Number the squares as on the half-sized plan (6.2). Using the squares as a guide, draw the half-shape of your guitar. Try to achieve a smooth, flowing curve without any bumps or flats. Cut out the shape with a coping-saw, then smooth the edge with a file and sanding sticks until there are no irregularities. It

6   THE MOULD

In its early stages of construction, a guitar is a very fragile and unstable object. It needs a sturdy support to hold everything rigid until it gradually attains a strength of its own. The Sides, having been bent to shape, try to straighten themselves out again if not held under restraint.

Some luthiers, after perhaps a lifetime's experience, make their guitars without the use of a mould. They work freely, using only a simple template to arrive at the shape they desire. It is obviously unthinkable for a beginner to try to emulate these master craftsmen, so I have designed a mould which will ensure complete success. You can make it entirely yourself with the exception of the bandsaw work, and it can be built from scrap timber if you have some available. Otherwise, 25mm chipboard is ideal.

Making a mould is laborious and time-consuming, but it is an essential part of the whole process of making your own guitar. Try to construct it with the same loving care that you will be lavishing on the instrument itself (6.1).

Materials

(1)   1 piece of 3mm hardboard, 50cm × 19cm.
(2)   4 pieces of 25mm chipboard, 61cm × 45cm.
(3)   2 softwood battens, 35cm × 5cm × 2cm.
(4)   4 pieces of dowel, 6cm × 15mm.
(5)   A piece of hardwood for wedges, 15cm × 45mm × 25mm.
(6)   Thirty-two 64mm, No. 10, steel, counter-sunk wood screws.
(7)   Sixteen 40mm, No. 8, counter-sunk wood screws.
(8)   A few 25mm panel pins.

The Template

The piece of hardboard has to be cut out to the exact half-shape of your guitar, and it becomes the template which is used to mark out the wood for the mould, the work board, and to outline the shape of the Sound-board and Back. Make certain that the hardboard is a

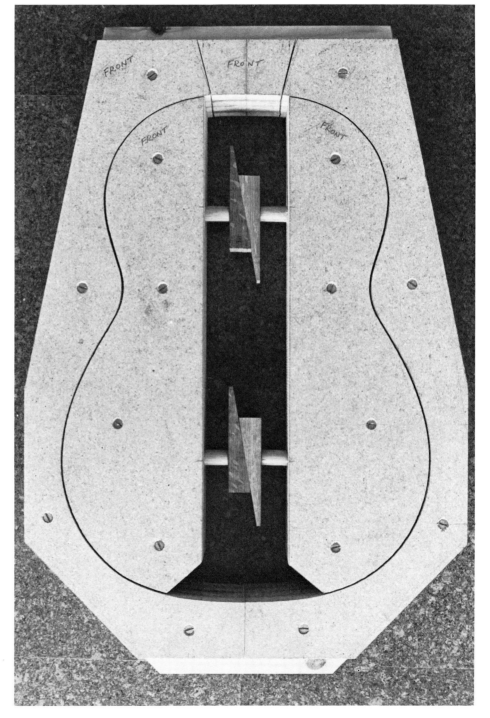

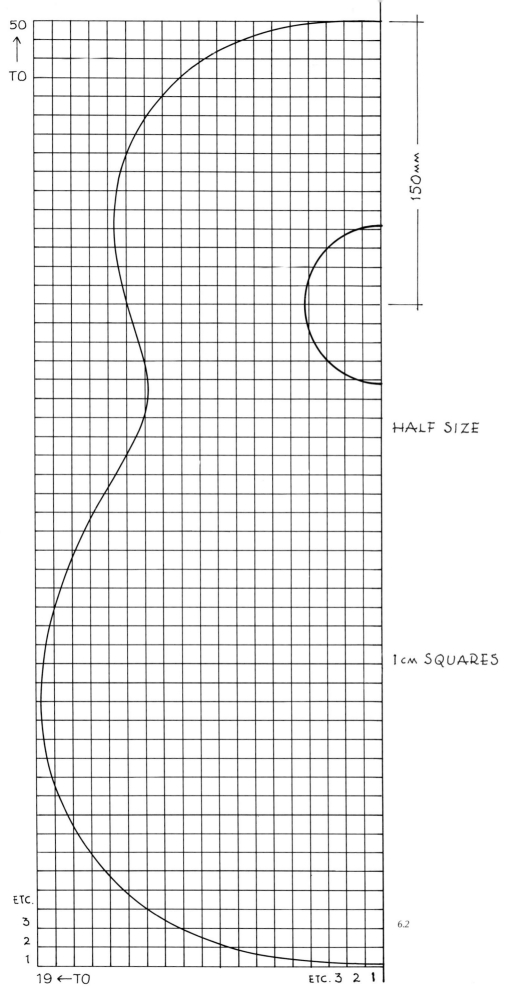

50
↑
TO

150mm

HALF SIZE

1 CM SQUARES

6.2

ETC.
3
2
1

19 ←TO

ETC. 3 2 1

is important that the shape is as near perfect as possible, so try it out by first drawing a centre-line on a large sheet of paper and then drawing round your template, turning it over to arrive at a symmetrical guitar shape. Check the top and bottom curves where they meet the centre-line, and adjust the shape of the template if there are bumps or flats at these points. When you are quite satisfied that no more improvements can be made you are ready to start making your mould.

Marking out the mould

1   Draw a true centre-line from top to bottom on one of your pieces of chipboard with a ball-point pen.

2   Place the edge of your template on the centre-line, making sure that the distances from top and bottom edges are equal.

3   Tack down the template lightly with two panel pins to prevent any possibility of movement, and draw round the half-shape.

4   Turn the template over and repeat 2 and 3 above to produce the complete shape for band-sawing (6.3).

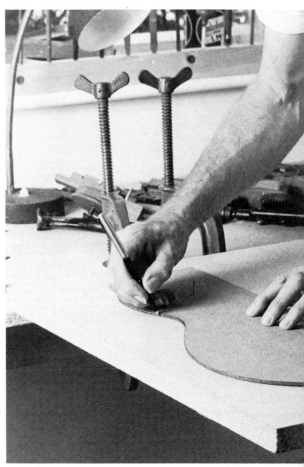

5 Draw the lines marking the waste-removal using the measurements shown on the drawing (6.4).

6 Make up a four-tier sandwich with the other three boards and clamp them together.

7 Drill pilot holes for the 32 No. 10 screws. When drilling for screws, always use two drills—one for the unthreaded part of the screw, or shank, which must be a fraction over-size, and one for the thread, considerably under-size. In this case, the correct drill sizes would be 4mm and 2mm. The screw-heads must be countersunk with a countersinking bit. Suggested positions for the screws are indicated by crosses on the drawing, but the important points to remember are to place the screws well away from the sawing lines and to make certain that opposing screws do not foul one another.

8 Screw all the boards together from both sides, remove the clamps, and have the mould sawn on a machine by a skilled band-saw operator (6.5). (Don't attempt to cut out the shape by hand because it would be impossible to keep the walls of the mould perpendicular). A timber merchant will tell you where

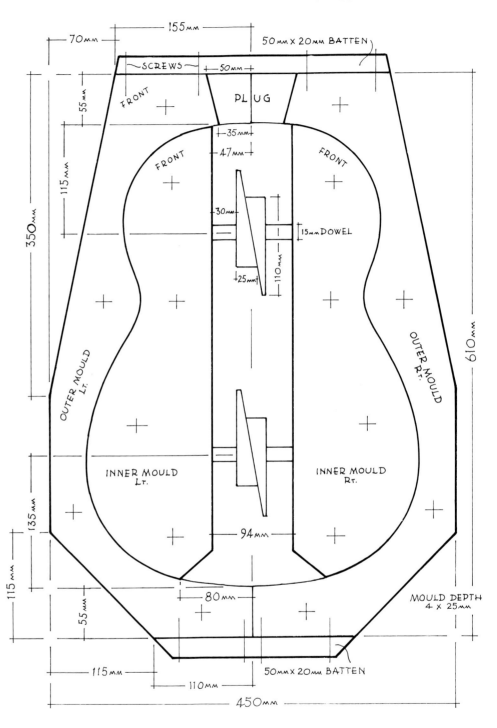

6.4

to find the best band-saw operator in your area. The first cut will be made on the centre-line, then the two halves forming the inner and outer moulds are cut out. Give instructions that the cut must be made on the inside of the line. Have all the waste wood cut away by machine with the exception of the gap for the Neck in the outer mould—you will remove this at a later stage by hand.

6.3 **Marking out the mould**

6.5 **The mould being band-sawn**

6.6 **Two pairs of folding wedges**

2   Glue together the *two inner layers only* in each half, with P.V.A. glue.

3   Screw on the top and bottom layers, locating the screws in their original holes. Wipe away squeezed-out glue. (These outside layers are removable to allow the Linings to be fitted and clamped later).

4   Drill and countersink the two end battens for the No. 8 screws where shown. Note that these battens are screwed to the inner layers only.

5   Hold the two halves of the outer mould tightly together on a flat surface, mark through the holes in the battens, drill small pilot holes in the mould, and then screw the battens on.

6   Mark out the gap for the Neck to pass through.

7   Remove the top batten and saw out the Neck gap with a tenon-saw. Keep the pieces in their correct order to form the plug.

8   Replace the top batten, locating the screws in their original holes.

9   Glue the plug together, clamping it until set.

10   Smooth out any irregularities on the inner faces of the mould.

Assembling the Inner Mould

1   Separate the layers, keeping the same order as before, and glue together the *two centre planks only* in each half with P.V.A. glue.

2   Screw on the top and bottom layers. These sections are removeable as in the outer mould.

3   Drill out the two holes in each half to receive the dowels. (These holes should be about 3cm deep).

4   Squeeze P.V.A. glue into the holes and knock in the four dowels with a wooden mallet. (The glue joining the two centre planks must be quite set, otherwise they will be forced apart by the dowels). If your dowels fit tightly, a hydraulic action takes place, preventing them from reaching the bottoms of the holes. The secret is to score a groove down the side of each dowel to allow the glue to escape.

5   Make the four folding wedges from the block of hardwood (which can be of beech or oak), by sawing diagonally and then lengthwise. The four wedges (6.6), must be planed and sanded smooth.

6   Assemble the complete mould by tapping in the wedges, and mark it clearly on the inner and outer moulds with the words FRONT and BACK.

Assembling the Outer Mould

1   Deal with the outer mould first. Separate all the layers, numbering them as you do so, and taking care to keep them in their original order.

PART 2

7 PREPARING THE SIDES

Having successfully completed all the preliminary tasks, you are now ready to start on the guitar itself. Everything has been leading up to this moment.

The first thing to do is to plane both surfaces of the two Sides.

1   Clamp each Side to the bench in turn, using a short batten across the end, and planing *away* from the clamp (7.1). If you attempt to plane against a bench-stop in the usual way, you will almost certainly fracture the thin plank. Remove as little wood as possible, with the smoothing plane set for a fine cut.

2   Turn the plank round and plane the other end. The book-matched Sides will have been sliced apart on a machine, leaving tool marks across the width of the planks. These ridges must be planed off.

3   Inspect the Sides very closely after smoothing and mark them clearly with a diagonal pencil line across the two matching faces, i.e. where the wood has been sliced apart. These surfaces will become the outside of

7.1 **Planing one of the Sides**

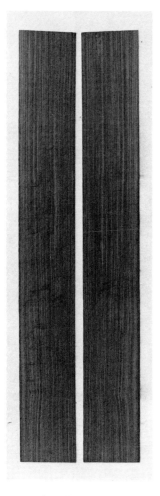

7.2 Matching the grain of the Sides

7.3 Scraping the Sides

your guitar, so it is important to get this right. You will see the grain matching in a perfectly symmetrical pattern (7.2).

4   Decide which two edges are to be uppermost (glued to the Sound-board), true them up if necessary with your longest plane, and measure off 10cm from the trued edges, across the ends of both planks. This will be the preliminary width for bending.

5   Saw off the excess carefully so that these long strips can be used for future Edgings.

Before the Sides can be bent to shape, they must be thinned down to their final thickness of 2mm.

6   Clamp the two Sides to the bench, side by side and face down, with a batten across the ends, making sure that they are both the same way round.

7   Plane the surfaces systematically, starting at one edge and moving across the planks with each successive stroke. This will ensure a uniform thickness. The fore plane or smoothing plane can be used, whichever you find the easiest to handle.

8   Unclamp the Sides when you reach the opposite edge, turn them round end for end, and plane them in the other direction.

9   Check the edge thickness all round, and when you have achieved an even thickness of about 2·5mm, commence using your thicknessing caliper (See

Chapter 16, Figure 16.2 on page 62. Set the gap of the caliper so that the wood just passes through at its thinnest point, and remove any 'high' spots marked with the pencil. Gradually decrease the gap of the caliper until it measures exactly 2mm. (A test piece of wood, 2mm thick, can be prepared rather like a mechanic's feeler-gauge, to check the gap).

If your plane is working well, and you feel confident of your skill, you can approach very closely to the finished thickness. Otherwise it is safer to change to the scraper. This is the tool to use in any case for the final thicknessing. Push the tool away from you in long, even strokes, working evenly across the surface as before (7.3).

Some makers reduce the Sides to about 1.5mm, particularly on their Flamenco models; the thinner wood produces the rather sharp, bright tone characteristic of this type of guitar. The slightly heavier classical guitar, however, really needs the extra half-millimetre for structural reasons. The important thing to aim for is evenness of thickness; a thin area will not only cause weakness and possible buckling of the Sides, but it can also be the cause of a poor response from some notes on the instrument. It is also of great importance that the two Sides should be of equal thickness, otherwise the tonal balance of the guitar will be upset.

With the Sides reduced to their final thickness, you are now ready to move on to the bending operation.

8 BENDING THE SIDES

The subtle curve of the Sides of a guitar is best achieved using only dry heat. It is not the easiest method to use, and many makers resort to other means of softening the timber, from gentle dampening to steeping for an hour or more in a vat of boiling water. The age-old method of heating the Sides on a hot pipe without previous soaking has always appealed to me because of the fact that excessive humidity is the enemy of all musical instruments. With rosewood in particular, it is best to use as little dampening as possible, because it contains oils and waxes which bring out in the timber its own special quality and beauty. Boiling, or soaking in hot water, is bound to remove some of these oils from deep inside the wood, with a consequent loss of quality. Makers generally agree, however, that any effect this would have on the eventual tone of the guitar would be difficult to prove.

The first thing is to decide which pair of ends will form the bottom of the guitar.

1   Match the grain symmetrically where the bottom joint will come.

2   Lay the Sides face down, side by side, and mark them clearly, 'top' and 'bottom'.

3   Pin a strip of stiff paper around the edge of your hardboard template so that it follows the curves. Cut off the excess at the ends, and mark them 'top' and 'bottom'.

4   Mark the strip clearly where the inmost turn of the waist will come.

5   Remove the strip and position it on one of the Sides allowing an equal amount of waste, top and bottom.

6   Mark the waist position with a soft pencil.

7   Mark the second Side from the first to keep them symmetrical. There is no need to indicate where the ends will come because their position will be decided after the Sides have been bent and fitted into the mould.

8.1 **Bending the waist**

Some makers prefer to taper the Sides before bending them, but there is a lot to be said for keeping the edges parallel at this stage.

8   Heat up your bending iron to a temperature just high enough to cause a drop of water (or a *wet* finger!) to sizzle.

9   Start bending the waist curve by pressing the outside face against the iron and rocking the wood to and fro with light pressure for a few seconds (*8.1*). Never hold the Side stationary in one position on the iron for too long, or you will scorch the wood.

10   Keep inspecting the results and moving the wood along a little at a time in both directions on either side of your pencil mark.

If there is any sign of darkening of the wood, scorching is taking place and you should protect the surface by holding a piece of dampened veneer between the iron and the Side.

8.2 **Making small adjustments to the curves**

11   Remove the wood from the iron every minute or two, holding it to shape and waving it up and down to cool it.

12   When you think you are approaching the correct shape, keep checking it against the mould as you work, then turn the Side over and begin bending the curve of the lower bout.
   The secret is to work slowly and with firm pressure, moving the wood constantly over the iron. Aim for a smooth, flowing curve rather than an exact match with the mould at this stage.

13   Bend the upper bout, and then start to fit the Side more accurately into the mould.

14   Place your mould face down on a flat board (with the inner mould removed), and keep trying the Side in it with the trued-up edge downwards, resting on the board. Make small adjustments to the curves on the iron, increasing the bend here, flattening it there, until it finally fits snugly all round (*8.2*).
   The waist is the trickiest part to bend, due to the sharpness of the curve. Keep a close watch for the slightest sign of cracking or buckling as you work, and stop immediately if it seems even remotely possible. If you feel that it is impossible to achieve the tight curve without risking fracture, you will have to dampen the wood in this area with a sponge. This is nearly always necessary when using rosewood, which has less flexibility than maple.

15   Curve the ends gently where they temporarily overlap the centre-line.

16   Bend the opposite Side in the same way (8.3), but remember that the Sides are 'left-handed' and 'right-handed'. If you get this wrong, the grain pattern will not match up at the bottom of your guitar. This point may seem obvious, but mistakes have been made, even by the most experienced luthiers.

It is a good idea to leave the wood to settle for a day or two after bending (8.4). When you try the Sides in the mould again you will probably find that they have straightened out a bit. This is easily rectified on the iron without the need to dampen the wood.

When you are quite satisfied that there are no flats or bumps which spoil the smoothness of the curves, move on to the next operation, which is fixing the Bottom Block.

8.4 **Giving the wood a rest**

8.3 **Bending the opposite Side**

33

9.1 **Fitting the inner mould sections**

9   THE BOTTOM BLOCK

Place the outer mould face down on a flat surface, and press one of your Sides in with its matching inner mould. You will find that slight adjustments to the curves of the inner mould will be necessary because the Sides are thicker than the original band-saw cut (9.1). Fit one mould-half at a time by carefully paring it down in the tight areas at the top and bottom with a surform and sanding stick until it will press snugly into the inside curve of the Side.

1   Saw the surplus off the Side at top and bottom, but leaving about 5mm overlapping the centre-line. Do the same with the other half, then clamp the Sides in tightly by tapping in the wedges.

2   Where the bottom waste portions overlap, mark the edges exactly on the centre-line with a Stanley

9.2 **The Sides butted together at the bottom**

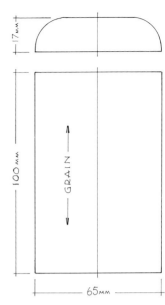

9.3 **The Bottom Block**

9.4 **Shaping the Block to the curve of the sides**

knife.

3   Turn the mould over and do the same on the other edges.

4   Remove the Sides from the mould and join up the marks across all faces of the Sides.

5   Cut off the waste with a fine-toothed saw, allowing a half millimetre or so for final fitting.

6   Clamp the Sides back in tightly, and inspect the fit. Gradually reduce the bottom ends, by trial and error, until they butt together with the wedges in firmly (9.2).

7   Make the Bottom Block to the measurements shown on the diagram (9.3), with the grain running from top to bottom. With the mould face down, the Block should stand above the level of the Sides by one millimetre or so to allow for the arch of the Back. (The Block will be 'faired in' at a later stage).

8   The back of the Block (its gluing surface) must be rounded slightly to fit the curve of the Sides. An easy way to achieve a good fit is to tape a piece of sandpaper to the Sides and rub the Block up and down against it (9.4).

9   Insert a piece of thin polythene between Sides and mould, and glue the Block in position with Cascamite. Cramp up, using softening-pads of wood to avoid

bruising the face of the Block (9.5).

10   Wipe away surplus glue with a damp cloth and leave overnight to harden.

9.5 **Gluing in the Bottom Block**

10.1 **The 'V' splice**

10.2 **The reversed scarf**

10.3 **Cutting the scarf**

14°

180 MM

14°

23½ MM

94 MM

86 MM

18 MM

178 MM

TO BE TRIMMED OFF

PLANE OFF

18 MM

FULL SIZE

10 NECK AND HEAD

The complete Neck, including the Head, Heel and Foot, could obviously be cut from a solid block of mahogany, but it would be very wasteful and the result would not be as strong as the built up assembly I will describe. You can buy partly formed neck-blanks, but these are too short for this method of construction.

The most convenient way to tackle the operation is to deal with the Head first. All the delicate work can be completed before joining the Neck to the Sides, leaving only the screwing on of the tuning machines after varnishing.

The traditional joint between Neck and Head is the 'V' splice (*10.1*). Unfortunately, it is a fiendishly difficult joint to make, and I would not advise the use of it on your first guitar unless you are already a highly skilled wood-worker. The best alternative is the reversed scarf joint (*10.2*). The decorative facing on the Head covers the end grain of the Neck, and all that remains visible is the glue line underneath the Head.

1   Make sure that your plank of mahogany conforms to the measurements given in Chapter 2 after smoothing and squaring up with a plane.

2 Draw a line right around the wood with a try-square 86mm from one end, then draw another line 94mm further down.

3 Draw a diagonal between these two lines on both edges of the wood as shown in 10.2.

4 Clamp the wood on edge and saw very carefully on the diagonal with a tenon saw (10.3).

5 Clamp the two pieces firmly together on the edge of the bench so that the diagonal faces are in line, and then plane them until they are flat and square. By placing a piece of softwood underneath, you will be able to plane a feather edge on the end of the Neck. The backing piece should be slightly wider, and must project a little beyond the Neck (10.4). Keep checking with a try-square to be certain of keeping the faces true in all directions.

6 Reverse the smaller piece which will become the Head and place it underneath the Neck to form the 14 degree angle between Head and Neck.

7 Cramp this assembly together on the bench before applying glue, using a similar arrangement to the one shown in 10.5. This is called 'cramping up dry'.

8 When you are certain that the joint can be held together firmly without the possibility of the angled pieces sliding on one another, unclamp and spread a thin layer of Araldite on both faces of the joint. Araldite

is recommended for this joint rather than Cascamite, not for reasons of strength, but because the glue-line under the Head will be less noticeable after varnishing.

9 Cramp up again, not forgetting to insert a piece of polythene between the joint and the bench, tightening the holding down cramps first to prevent sliding. (Always insert small pieces of softwood or hardboard under the cramp heads.)

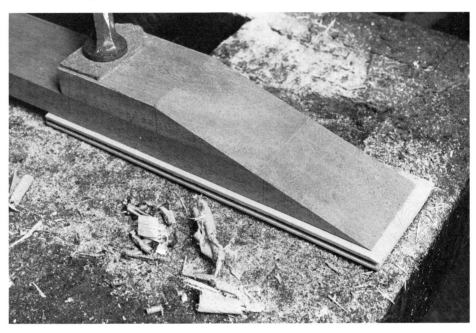

10.4 **Truing the scarf**

10.5 **Gluing the joint**

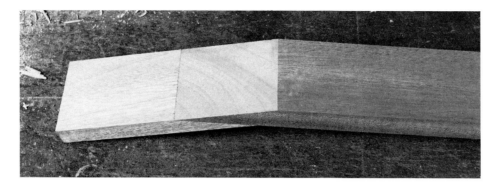

10 Remove any surplus glue that has squeezed out of the joint, and leave for 12 hours at room temperature to harden. (Allow a longer time to set if you are working in colder conditions.)

Assemble the pieces of veneer with which you intend to face the Head. Alternating layers of dark and light woods create a pleasing effect on all the edges after shaping and drilling. Rosewood veneer makes a very attractive facing for the Head, and I have used a four-tier sandwich of rosewood and sycamore. It is really a matter of personal taste and the availability of decorative veneers. Some makers express their individuality quite freely in their Head design and this feature becomes their form of signature. Strips of mosaic inlay to match the Sound-hole decoration are sometimes let into the facing, and the top of the Head can be shaped to your own design. The possibilities are endless, but over-elaboration should be avoided; simplicity is the essence of good style.

11 Clean up your reversed scarf joint with a smoothing plane, and then reduce the thickness of the Head (10.6). Use a marking gauge set to 18mm to give you a line to plane down to, then clamp the Neck to the bench with the Head-blank projecting over the edge, enabling the face to be planed.

12 Measure 42cm down the face of the Neck-blank from the angle with the Head, and saw off this end piece which will later form the Heel and Foot.

13 Cut rectangles of veneer allowing 5mm or so all round for trimming.

10.6 **The Head-blank reduced to the correct thickness**

10.7 **Veneering the face of the Head**

10.8 **The overlapping edges of the veneer planed off**

14   Spread P.V.A. glue on the face of the Head and lay on the first veneer. Brush on more glue and follow with the succeeding layers as quickly as possible. Cramp the Head face down on a flat surface, interposing a sheet of thin polythene or grease-proof paper. Take care when cramping that you protect the back of the Head with a piece of hardboard, and also that the layers of veneer are not allowed to slide out of place on the wet glue (*10.7*). Make sure there is plenty of overlap at the angle between Head and Neck.

15   After about an hour the overlapping edges of veneer can be planed off flush with the Head. This reveals the decorative effect of the successive layers (*10.8*). The top end can be left rough at this stage, but the lower edge must be cut exactly on the angle between the Head and Neck. The best way to achieve a clean edge here, is to make a cut with a Stanley knife against a try-square. Then, with a paring chisel, cut a shallow groove on the waste side. Run your fine backsaw in this groove. Note that the resulting cut must be perpendicular to the face of the Neck. The Fingerboard will later be glued 5mm away from this edge, forming a slot into which the ivory Nut is fitted.

16   Cut out an accurate cardboard template to the measurements given in *10.9*, and including your Head shape. There is no need to cut out the string slots on the template—just prick through the centres of the drill holes at both ends of each slot.

17   Draw a centre-line along the Neck and Head on the front and back surfaces, and lightly cramp the template in position on the face of the Head. Draw round it with a sharp pencil, pricking through the centres of the holes with the point of a pair of compasses (*10.10*). Do the same on the back of the Head, by laying your template to a line marked round the Head from the top of your design on the front.

18   Drill a 2.5mm pilot hole through the four centre points at the ends of the string slots. If you have no

access to a vertical drill-press, enter the Head from each side, meeting in the middle.

19   Slide the drilling-guide (featured in Chapter 4) on to your 16mm bit, locate the point in a pilot hole at the

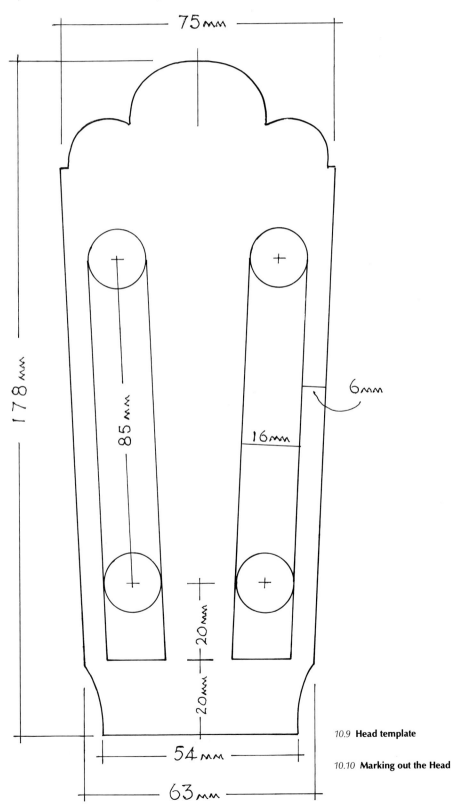

10.9 **Head template**

10.10 **Marking out the Head**

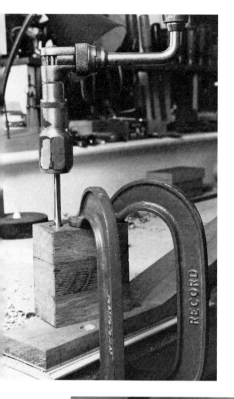

back of the Head, and clamp the guide and Head to a planed piece of softwood (*10.11*). It is very important to provide this smooth, flat surface for the Head-facing to rest on, because the four holes are drilled right through from the back, resulting in a clean hole in the veneer facing.

20   Cut out the Head shape on the waste side of the line with a tenon saw and coping saw.

21   Before cutting out the slots, drill the holes to receive the rollers of the tuning-machines. To mark the positions of the holes accurately you will have to use your tuning-machine side-plates as templates, because the distance between the rollers varies slightly with different makes. Remove the six screws fastening the rollers to the cogs (put the screws, rollers and cogs safely in a small container), and after planing the sides of the Head smooth and square, mark through the roller holes in the side-plates to give the exact position for drilling (*10.12*). Make certain that you position the side-plates on their correct sides of the Head; the tuning button with its worm drive comes above the cog-wheel.

23   Re-assemble the tuning-machines and test their fit in the holes. If necessary, drill out more wood until the side-plates touch the Head, then go a millimetre deeper for clearance.

24   Remove the waste from the string slots with a coping saw or a frame-saw (after releasing one end of the blade and passing it through one of the holes).

25   Finalise the shaping of the Head by cleaning up all the edges, using chisels, files and sanding sticks. The edges of the veneer are very fragile and easily chipped. Always cut, file or sand inwards from the face with single, forward strokes of the tool.

26   The lower ends of the string-slots are shaped to form a free exit for the strings. This clearance ramp can be either flat-based or rounded according to personal preference. If you decide on a flat one, make sloping saw cuts with a fine back-saw at the sides of the slots and then chisel out the waste (*10.14*). Use the decorative layers of veneer as a cutting guide, so that they form even lines, parallel with the cut end of the facing (*10.15*). If you choose a rounded ramp, use your round-sectioned file and sanding sticks (*10.16*).

10.11 Drilling out the ends of the string slots

10.12 Marking the positions of the roller holes

10.13 Drilling the roller holes

22   Grip the Head in a vice and drill the six holes with an 11mm bit at exactly a right-angle with the sloping sides. A try-square can be rested on the Head to keep the bit upright. Drill very slowly, pausing to sight from all angles to ensure that the holes will be true. For greater accuracy, the drilling-guide can be used again by drilling an 11mm hole through it. The Head and guide can be clamped to the bench using a suitably tapered resting-piece (*10.13*). A strip of adhesive tape wrapped round the bit provides a simple depth gauge.

10.14 Cutting square string
clearance ramps

10.16 **An example of rounded
ramps on a head by Harald
Petersen**

10.15 **The finished Head**

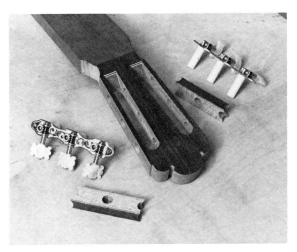

11 HEEL AND FOOT

There are two generally accepted methods of fixing the Neck to the Sides. One way entails gluing in a Top Block, rather like the Bottom Block but on a larger scale. The Neck is then dovetailed into this Block. As you can imagine, this joint is very difficult to make accurately by hand. It is used mainly in the mass production industry where most of the guitar-making operations are mechanised. Some distinguished luthiers, however, use the dovetail or 'European' method.

The other way is known as the 'Spanish method'. The main difference is that no separate Top Block is used; instead, the Neck, Head, Heel and Foot are constructed as one unit, and the Sides are glued into slots cut in the Heel. This is the method I will describe.

11.1 **Gluing the Heel and Foot laminations**

11.3 **Sawing the slots for the Sides**

1   Cut the spare piece of Neck wood into three equal parts, each 14cm long. These pieces must now be glued together on the end of the Neck to form a laminated blank from which the Heel and Foot will be carved.

2   Glue them all face to face on the underside of the Neck with Cascamite, and clamp them down very firmly to squeeze out the surplus glue. This will ensure that the joins between the layers are almost invisible. If you use a clamping arrangement similar to the one illustrated in *11.1*, the laminations will be prevented from slipping out of alignment.

3   Leave this laminated blank to set completely (preferably overnight), before removing the cramps, then plane the sides flat and square with the Neck.

4   Draw all the centre-lines and outlines of the Neck, Heel and Foot as accurately as possible on the wood, using the measurements given in *11.2* overleaf.

5   Cut the slots to receive the Sides first. Take special note that these slots do not enter squarely into the Heel because the Sides are slightly curved where they come together. Make your saw-cuts at an angle of two degrees to the line across the Neck to allow for this curve. (If you start your cut 1·5mm back from the guide-line, it will work out correctly. (See *11.2*.)

The slots should be just under 2mm wide to accommodate the Sides, and if you are an expert in saw setting, you can set the teeth of a saw to provide this width of cut without more ado. Otherwise, the slots can be very accurately cut with a fine backsaw or tenon saw in the following way. Dealing with one slot at a time, make cuts with a Stanley knife on the pencil lines marking the position, angle, and width of the slot. Now cut 'V' shaped grooves with the corner of a chisel in the waste portion alongside the knife cuts. Run a fine saw in

the groove, watching carefully to make certain that the saw is following your guide lines on the top face of the Neck, and on the base of the Heel. Saw very slowly, especially when nearing the bottom of the slot. Note carefully from the diagram that the slots are deeper at the base of the Heel than on the face of the Neck.

Now make a second saw-cut in the same way, a little less than 2mm from the previous one. If you push a piece of veneer into your first cut, the saw will be prevented from wandering back into it (*11.3*). Proceed with the other side, and then clear the slots with a fine chisel (you can make one from a small file). Make sure that the ends of the slots are equidistant from the centre-lines, and that the bottom of each slot is straight.

6   Clamp the blank to the bench and remove the bulk of the waste wood from the Foot and the Heel with a tenon saw and frame-saw (*11.4* and *11.5*).

7   Saw off the long pieces at each side of the Neck, but keep the saw-cut well clear of the line—about 1·5mm (*11.6*).

8   Finish the Foot by shaping with files, smoothing with sanding sticks, and rounding all the corners as in *11.10*.

11.4 **Roughing out the Foot**

11.5 **Cutting out the profile of the Heel**

11.6 **The bulk of the waste wood removed**

HALF SIZE ~ MEASUREMENTS IN MMS

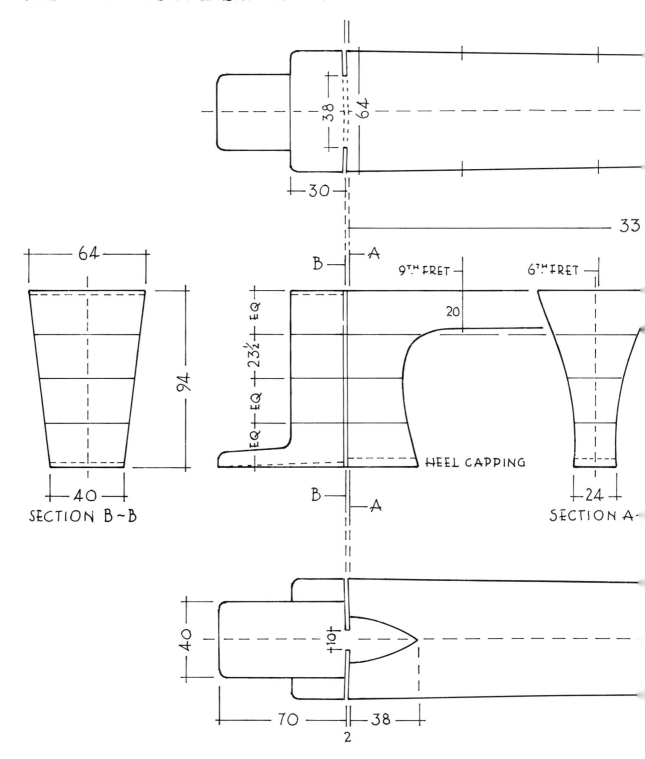

SECTION B~B

SECTION A~

HEEL CAPPING

9TH FRET   6TH FRET

11.2

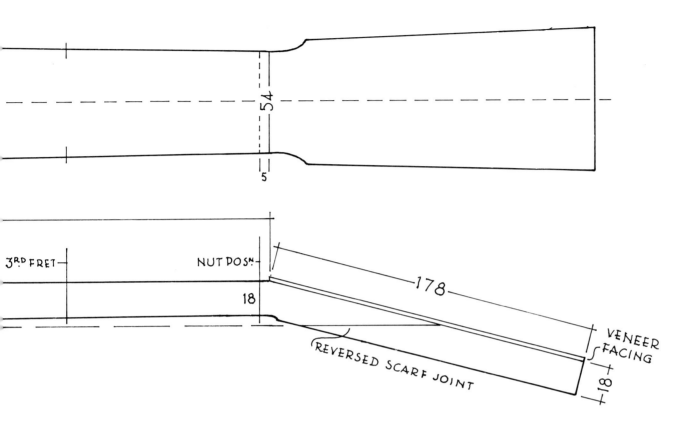

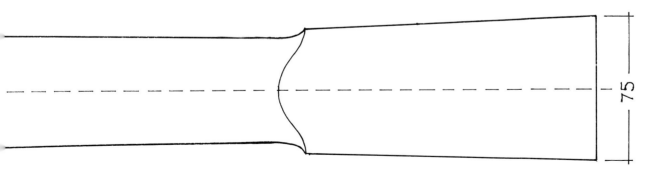

11.7 **Carving the Heel**

11.8 **Approaching the final shape**

11.9 **Templates for shaping the Heel**

FULL SIZE

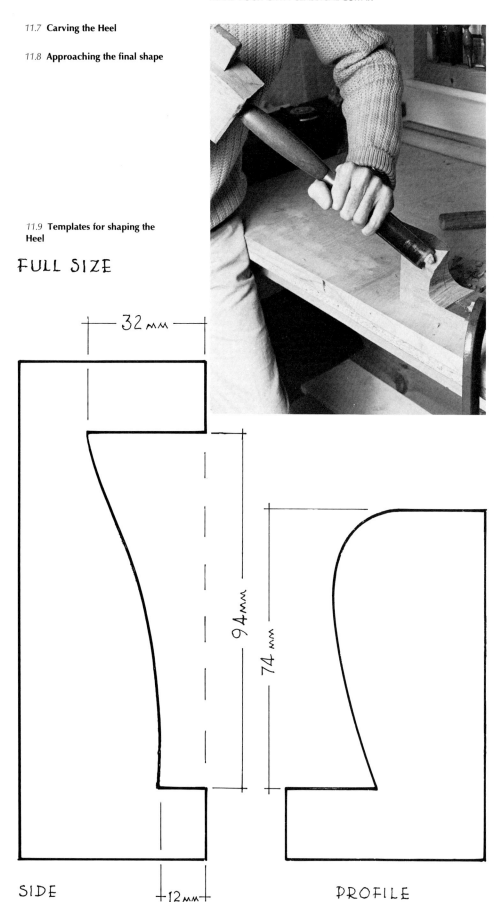

32 мм

94мм

74 мм

SIDE 12мм PROFILE

9   Clamp the blank firmly on the bench and carve the Heel with a large gouge struck with a wooden mallet (11.7). Remove progressively smaller pieces of wood as you approach the final shape (11.8), changing to a smaller gouge used with hand pressure only. Use both hands on the chisel, one applying the cutting force and the other guiding the tool. Your gouges must be razor-sharp so that the minimum amount of pressure is needed; the cuts will then be clean. If you have never used a gouge in this way before, it would be advisable to practise on an off-cut of mahogany. Carve the Heel to within 1.5mm of the finished outline of the Neck. This spare wood must be retained to allow for final shaping after the Finger-board has been glued on.

10   Make a cardboard half-template, as in 11.9, and use it constantly to ensure that the contour of the Heel where it will meet the Sides, is symmetrical, and that it follows a smooth curve. The underside of the Neck is left unshaped until the Finger-board has been glued on and fretted, so that a flat, clamping surface is provided.

After smoothing with files and sandpaper, the Heel and Foot are ready to receive the Sides (11.10 and 11.11).

11.10 **The Heel and Foot ready for the Sides**

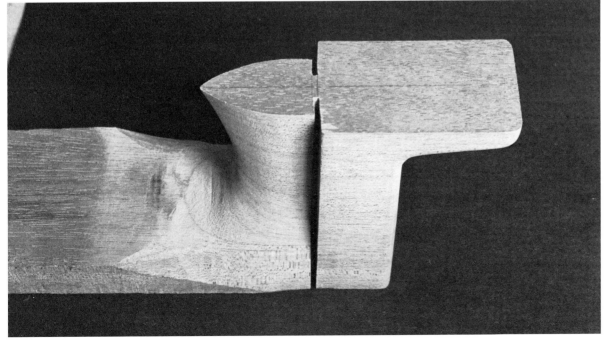

11.11 **The ends of the slots in the Heel**

3 On the base of the Heel, and on the face of the Neck, measure with a pair of dividers or compasses, the distance from the centre-line to the bottoms of the slots, transferring these measurements to the Sides (12.1). When transferring the measurement at the base of the Heel, don't forget to place it on your 94mm mark.

12 FITTING THE NECK

The Sides must now be fitted tightly into the slots cut in the Heel. It is not a lengthy operation but it has to be performed with great care because the Neck must be set in exact alignment with the body of the instrument. Also, the external appearance of your guitar will be affected by the quality of the joint between the Neck and the Sides.

The complete fitting and gluing operation can be carried out with the Sides clamped safely in the mould.

1 Mark and cut the overlapping Sides to form an accurate butt joint exactly on the centre-line in the same way that you fitted the Bottom Block.

2 Mark the position of the base of the Heel and Foot on the inside of the Sides. This should be 94mm from the top edge.

12.1 **Marking the Sides in preparation for fitting the Neck**

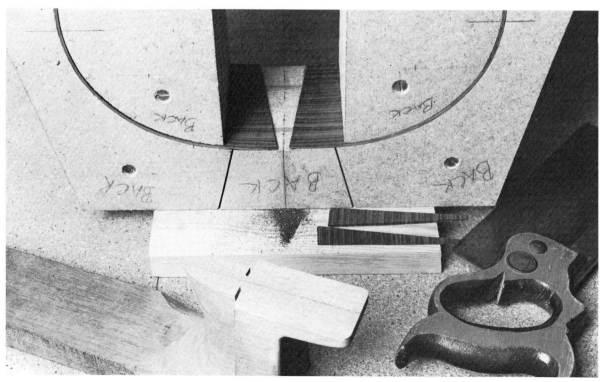

12.2 **Two equal segments sawn off**

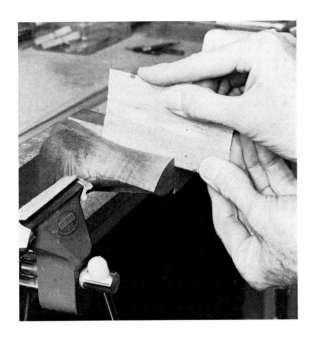

4   Using a Stanley knife and steel rule, join these points with diagonal lines across the Sides, and saw off the waste segments (12.2).

5   Remove the plug from the mould, and try the Sides in the slots. You are very lucky indeed if they fit! Widen the slots a little at a time, being careful not to round the sharp edges on the Heel, as this would spoil the closeness of the joint. A good tool for widening the slots is a piece of aluminium sheet, about the size of a cabinet scraper, with fine aluminium-oxide paper glued to each side (12.3). A small, thin file would be equally effective.

6   When the Sides are almost filling their slots, taper the ends gradually with fine sandpaper until they just reach the bottoms of the slots.

7   Rule a long straight line on your flat work-board, and mark the width of the Neck at the Nut position at one end.

8   Apply Cascamite to the slots and Sides with a small brush, and with the assembled mould and Sides front uppermost, slide the Neck into place. Turn the mould over and press the Neck down (on to a piece of greaseproof paper) to ensure that the front of the mould and face of the Neck are quite level.

9   Line the assembly up on your guide-line (using the centre-lines on the Bottom Block and Top Block), making sure that the Head veneer is overlapping the edge of the board. (This is very important, otherwise the Neck will be given a downward tilt in relation to the body.) Check the alignment of the Neck at the Nut

position on your pencil marks, and clamp the mould and Neck to the work-board as shown in 12.4, until the glue has set. If your bench runs along a wall, raise the complete assembly on some large wood-blocks or a wooden box, so that the clamps will clear the bench top.

10   Wipe off surplus glue with a damp cloth.

12.4 **Sides and Neck clamped in alignment**

12.3 **Widening the slots**

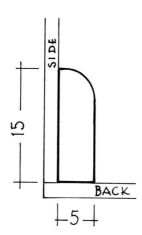

SECTION OF CONTINUOUS LINING

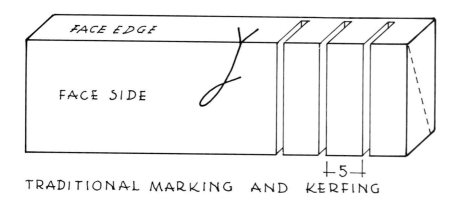

FACE EDGE

FACE SIDE

TRADITIONAL MARKING AND KERFING

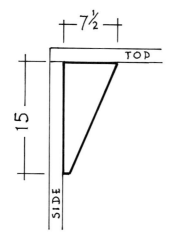

SECTION OF KERFED LINING

13   THE LININGS

The Bottom Lining

The 2mm thickness of the Sides would be insufficient for gluing on the Sound-board and Back. In any case, this small area is later reduced even further when the Edgings and Purflings are fitted, so in order to provide an adequate gluing surface, flexible strips of wood are added around all four inside edges of the Sides. These are called Linings. Fit the Bottom Lining first. This is made in two continuous strips.

1   Prepare the two strips of Lining wood by planing them to the section shown in 13.1. To do this accurately, first plane the face, and then the edge at a right-angle to it. To avoid snapping the thin strips whilst planing, grip one end with a cramp, and plane towards the free end. Mark the face and edge in the traditional way (13.1). Mark the exact finished thickness of the Linings (5mm) with a marking gauge and plane off the waste. Gauge the width (15mm) and plane down to the line in the same way.

2   Clamp each Lining strip in turn to the edge of the bench and round off one corner with a block plane as shown in 13.1. Smooth the strips with a sanding block.

3   Unscrew the back sections of the inner and outer moulds and remove them.

4   The measurements shown on the drawing (13.2)

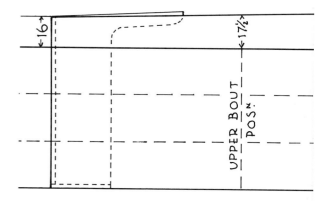

must be marked on the projecting Sides at the bottom joint, lower bout, waist, upper bout, and Heel.

5   Plane the Sides down to these marks with a block plane. The Heel and Foot must be reduced at the same time. A paring chisel is the best tool to use.

6   Shape the Foot to take the domed Back, curving it down towards the Sides as shown in *13.2*.

7   Reduce the height of the Heel to the level of the Sides, but keeping it horizontal. Finish off with a sanding stick (*13.3*).

8   The ends of the Linings are now notched 5mm into the Foot and the Bottom Block (*13.4* and *13.5*). Some makers dispense with this and butt the ends of the Linings against the Blocks. In my opinion the notched Linings are necessary for strength, because butt jointing, especially on the end-grain, is the weakest joint in carpentry. Mark the notches using the ends of the Linings as a guide, and cut them out with a small chisel.

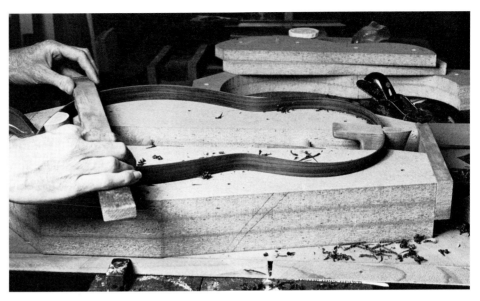

13.5 **Notches in the Bottom Block**

13.3 **Levelling the edges**

13.4 **Notches for the Linings in the Foot**

PROJECTING SIDES

19

22

25

WAIST POS.ⁿ

LOWER BOUT POS.ⁿ

BOTTOM BLOCK

3ᴿᴰ

2ᴺᴰ

MOULD 1ˢᵀ LAYER

13.2 **Tapering the Sides**

9 Heat up your bending iron and bend the Linings to conform to the inside curve of the Sides (13.6).

13.6 **Bending the Bottom Lining**

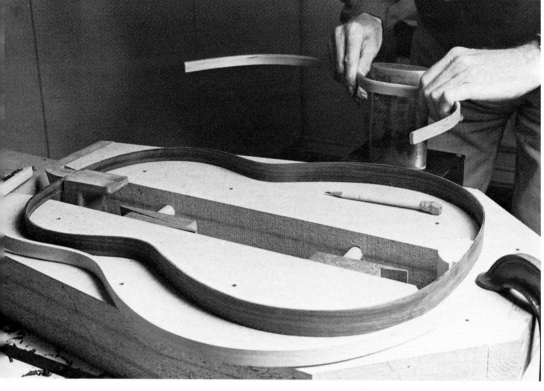

10 With the mould and Neck clamped firmly on the centre-line, fit the Linings dry, starting in the area of the waist. Make minor adjustments to the curve as you go along, and clamp the Linings to the Sides with clothes-pegs (13.7). The grip of the pegs can easily be strengthened by binding an elastic band around them. Cut off the ends so that they fit neatly into the notches. Inspect the Linings closely. If there are gaps, more careful bending is required. Time spent at this stage will be well rewarded when gluing.

11 Glue the Linings in with Cascamite (mixed slightly thicker than normally), so that they are projecting just above the Sides by about ½mm. Clamp them liberally with clothes-pegs all round. Squeeze out as much glue as possible with finger pressure.

12 Wipe away all excess glue with a damp cloth, being particularly careful to prevent it from running down between the Sides and the inner mould. Leave overnight in a temperature above 15°C before removing the clothes-pegs.

13 Replace the outer mould sections.

This completes the Bottom Lining. The slight (½mm) projection above the Sides is to allow for the fitting of the domed Back.

13.7 **The Bottom Linings clamped in**

The Top Lining

The majority of classical guitars are made with a 'kerfed' Top Lining. Kerfing is the process of making numerous saw-cuts 5mm apart, and part-way through the Lining strips. This not only makes the strips flexible without dampening or heating, but it is believed that it also improves the tone of the instrument. In effect, with a kerfed Lining, the Sound-board is held on by dozens of little triangular blocks, and the theory is that this form of construction gives it more freedom to vibrate. Some makers, in fact, glue lots of individual blocks all around the inside angle between the Sound-board and the Sides. The renowned luthier Hermann Hauser, however, fitted smooth continuous Linings, top and bottom, to many of his beautiful guitars, so the value of kerfing from a tonal point of view is questionable. Certainly, the fewer angles and corners inside the sound-chest, the smaller are the chances of setting up unwanted tonal reactions. I will later describe the fitting of a kerfed Top Lining so that you can decide which method you prefer.

Before you begin, the Top Block must be reduced in height by 2mm. This is to allow the Sound-board (which will be 2mm thick) to lie flush with the surface of the Neck. The edges of the Sides are then tapered back to the height of the Bottom Block.

14   Turn the mould over and clamp it accurately on the centre-line as before, only this time the Neck must be supported on pieces of scrap timber of the correct height, so that it is not strained out of true (up or down) when you clamp it to the work-board. Use a long straight-edge to test the alignment of the Neck in both directions; the centre-line down the face of the Neck must run true to the centre mark on the Bottom Block, also the face of the Neck must be level with the top of the Bottom Block.

15   Remove the front sections of the inner and outer moulds.

16   Make a Stanley knife-cut across the Neck where it joins the Sides, and cut a groove, 2mm deep, on the top of the Block with a chisel.

17   Gauge a pencil line around the top of the Block with a pair of compasses set at 2mm.

18   Pare off the waste from the Block with a chisel (13.8).

13.8 **Reducing the height of the Top Block**

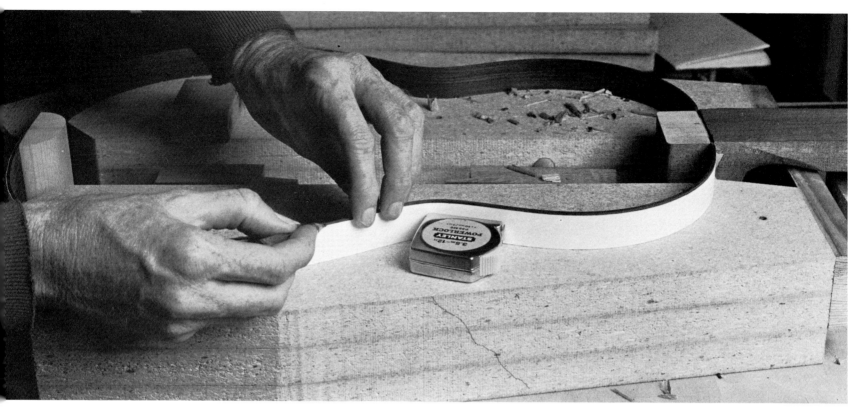

13.9 **Marking the amount of taper before fitting the Top Lining**

19   Cut a strip of stiff paper with a knife and straight-edge the same width as the projecting Side, and long enough to follow the curves of one Side from Neck joint to bottom joint. Measure 2mm from the edge at one end and join this mark with the edge at the other end. Cut off the taper, and fasten the strip to the Side with adhesive tape as shown in 13.9.

20   Draw a line on the projecting Side along the edge of the paper.

21   Plane down to the line, and repeat the procedure on the other Side. Test the level of the Sides with a straight-edge.

The very slight angle created in this way, between the top surface of the Neck and the Sound-board, produces a rise of the Finger-board of about 3mm at the Nut. A buzz-free action of the strings is therefore achieved without the need to taper the Finger-board, and an untapered Finger-board provides maximum reinforcement for the Neck.

A kerfed Lining is shaped slightly differently (13.1). It is triangular in section, but the kerfing is done before it is shaped. An ordinary mitre-box is used, as shown in 13.10. A vertical line is drawn 5mm to the right of the 90 degree saw guide, and each kerf is set against this line as a guide for the next cut. A tenon saw is used, and a strip

13.10 **Kerfing the Top Lining**

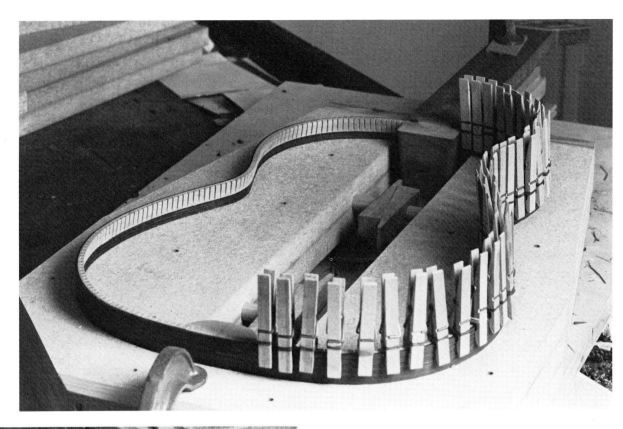

13.11 **The Top Lining fitted**

of soft metal such as brass, zinc, or aluminium, 1mm thick, provides the depth gauge. When both Lining strips have been kerfed, plane them to their triangular section on the edge of the bench with a block plane, and finish them with a sanding block. The individual kerfs may need to be cleaned up with a folded strip of sandpaper. The ends are again let into 5mm deep notches cut in the Blocks and shaped to the section of the Lining.

As mentioned earlier, a kerfed Lining should bend fairly easily to the curve of the Sides without resorting to the bending iron (13.11). Don't worry, though, if breakages occur on the sharper curves of the waist when you are fitting the strips; you can glue the pieces together later, clamping them tightly to the Sides. Don't hesitate to use a small metal cramp here and there (protecting the Sides with a piece of cardboard), if the clothes-pegs prove too weak for the job. Use Cascamite again, and be careful that the Linings do not slip down below the edges of the Sides; they should project very slightly as before. Remember to wipe away all the excess glue.

14 PREPARING THE SOUND-BOARD

This chapter and the two which follow, dealing with the construction of the Sound-board, are the most important in the book. The final quality of your guitar depends to a large extent on the patience and effort you lavish on this vital component. First of all, spend some time studying, tapping and gently flexing your two matched pieces of radially sawn spruce; in other words, get to know them thoroughly because they are very special pieces of wood. If you love the sight and feel of this beautiful material, your attitude towards it will affect the manner in which you work on it.

14.1 Planing the spruce for the Sound-board

1   Lay the two halves on the bench face up and edge-to-edge. Obviously, there are four different ways of doing this, but there is only one correct way. Probably your supplier will have marked the faces but to be certain that you have it right (and that *he* has it right!), put the boards together as they were in their original state (before being sliced apart). Open them out like the pages of a book in such a way that the edges with the closest grain come together in the centre of the Sound-board. Mark the faces of the boards in the waste area at one end with a soft pencil line across the touching edges, so that you can easily identify them.

2   Fix a thin batten (roughly half the thickness of your spruce) across the left-hand end of your bench with small panel pins. This will be your bench-stop for planing the boards. If the top of your bench is uneven or badly scored, clamp a flat work-board to it and pin your batten to this.

3   Sharpen your plane-iron (see Chapter 3).

4   Plane the backs of both boards first, completely removing all the saw marks (*14.1*). If the blade wants to dig into the surface rather than cut smoothly, turn the boards round and plane in the opposite direction. Set the plane-iron to cut more finely as work proceeds, so that you produce a satin smooth finish. Remove the minimum amount of wood to arrive at this end result. Final thicknessing is done after jointing and inlaying the Rosette, and will be dealt with in Chapter 16.

5   Inspect your bench-top to make certain that it is perfectly clean and smooth before turning the boards over. Spruce is soft, and indentations are difficult to remove.

6   Plane the faces, again removing as little wood as necessary to remove all flaws. Mark the faces for identification.

7   With the boards face up, find a matching pair of grain-lines that have a clear run from end to end, as near as possible to the inner edges. Mark these lines at each end on both boards. This is where your centre joint will come, and if you match the grain carefully the joint will be almost invisible.

8   Grip each board in the vice in turn, using pieces of felt or soft cardboard to protect the delicate surfaces, and plane the edges down to the marked grain-line.

9   Clean off the faces with a soft cloth, and clamp the boards face to face with a small cramp at each end. Make sure that the planed edges are absolutely level with each other. Now grip the whole assembly in the vice.

10   With razor-sharp fore-plane set fine, take a long, even shaving from the edges (*14.2*). Unclamp the boards, place them edge to edge, and inspect the joint against a strong light. If you can see light coming through, plane off another shaving. Continue in this way until you have produced a 'light-proof' joint. The joint in the upper half of the Sound-board is not as important as the lower half because of the position of the Finger-board and Sound-hole, so concentrate all your efforts on obtaining the closest possible join in the lower half. You may need to unclamp the boards to inspect your progress many times before you are completely satisfied. Leave the outside edges unplaned—this will immediately identify your jointing edges. Using the technique described above, the face of the jointed Sound-board will be flat even if your planing of the edges was not precisely square with the face (*14.3*). A shuting-board is not strictly necessary.

Gluing the Joint

Having achieved a close fitting butt joint between the two halves, lose no time in getting to grips with the gluing operation. The edges will change slightly if you leave them for too long, and you will have to true them up again.

There are many different ways of cramping up a glued, edge-to-edge joint, from adhesive tape, to complicated jigs. If you own, or can borrow a pair of cabinet makers' sash cramps (*14.4*), they should be used with care, weighting the boards down to a flat surface to prevent them from springing up when the sideways pressure is applied. Another way is to make a simple jig into which the boards fit (*14.5*), putting on the pressure with folding wedges. Whichever method you choose, test it thoroughly before mixing the glue, then you will be familiar with the procedure.

11   Clean the surface of your flat work-board in readiness for the clamping operation.

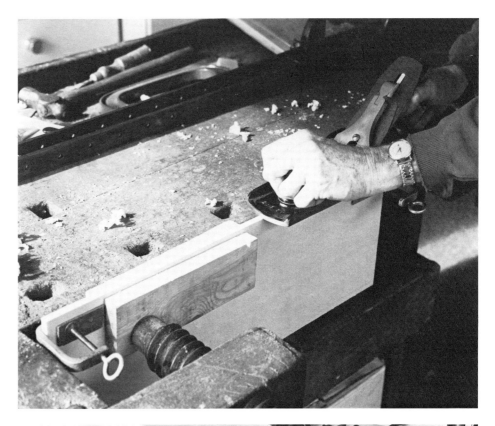

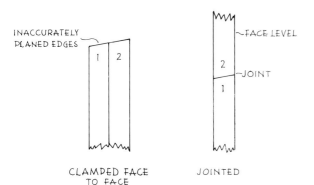

14.3   END VIEW OF BOARDS

14.2 **Jointing. Planing the edges**

14.4 **Jointing. Cramping up the Sound-board**

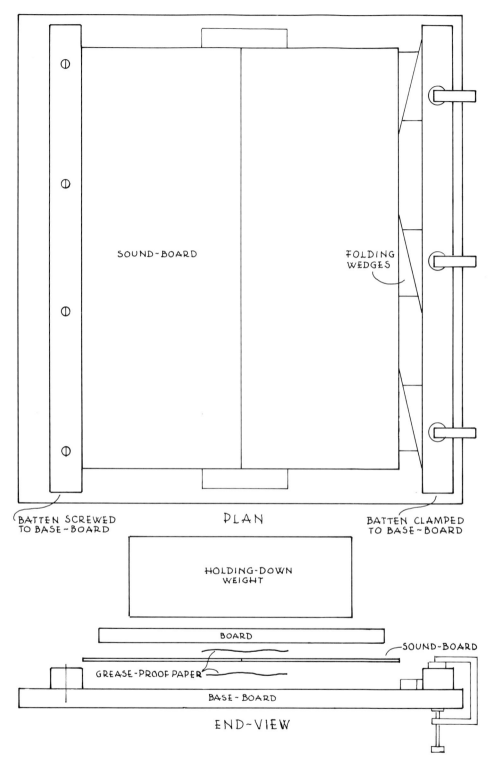

SOUND-BOARD

FOLDING
WEDGES

BATTEN SCREWED
TO BASE-BOARD

PLAN

BATTEN CLAMPED
TO BASE-BOARD

HOLDING-DOWN
WEIGHT

BOARD

SOUND-BOARD

GREASE-PROOF PAPER

BASE-BOARD

END-VIEW

14.5 **Jointing jig**

12 Place a strip of grease-proof paper on the board where the joint will come, and have another strip ready with which to cover the joint.

13 Apply Cascamite to both jointing edges, and press the boards together on the paper with hand pressure, sliding them up and down to squeeze out most of the glue. This is known as a 'rubbed' joint.

14 Cover the joint with the other strip of paper, place a weight on top (a tool box or the mould), and apply the pressure. Don't overdo the pressure, or you may distort your Sound-board.

Leave them for six hours at a room temperature of at least 15°C, or preferably overnight. It is *very important* to remember to release the cramping pressure *before* taking off the holding-down weight. If you forget to do this, the Sound-board will spring upwards, possibly breaking the joint.

Clean up the joint on both sides of the Sound-board with a plane or scraper. Your joint should be just visible as a hair-line down the centre of the board.

If you are not quite satisfied with the result, separate the boards with a tenon saw, and start again from Instruction 7. It is well worth the extra time and effort to make this joint as near perfect as you can. Make certain, though, that you will have sufficient width of spruce remaining to accommodate the lower bout before embarking on a re-jointing session.

15 THE ROSETTE

When I was contemplating building my first guitar, the thing which terrified me most of all was the Rosette inlaying. The very thought of cutting into that perfect surface and gluing in a complicated pattern of coloured woods kept me awake at night! But, as with most of these problems, after breaking the operation down into simple steps, I was able to produce an almost perfect inlay at the first attempt. I cheated a bit, though—and I advise you to do the same for your first guitar—I bought a ready-made Rosette ring. If the idea of designing and building up a pattern of your own excites you, however, turn to the end of this chapter.

1   Plane both surfaces of the spruce Sound-board, thinning it down to about 2 ½ to 3mm. This is only a preliminary thicknessing, and it is sufficient at this stage to check the thickness on the edges with a rule. Make certain that the surfaces are flat by testing with a straight-edge.

2   Lay your template on the face of the Sound-board, lining it up with the centre joint, and draw round the shape leaving some waste at the top and bottom. Don't cut it out at this stage.

3   Mark the centre of the Sound-hole on the joint using the measurement given in Chapter 6, Figure 6.2.

4   With a pair of pencil compasses set to a radius of 42mm, draw the Sound-hole circle.

5   Lay your Rosette ring in position accurately, and mark the inside and outside edges on the Sound-board with a Stanley knife at one point only. There is no need to draw round the ring. There should be a margin of spruce about 2mm wide around the edge of the Sound-hole.

6   Tack the Sound-board down firmly around all its edges to a flat board, and drill an 8mm hole exactly in the centre of the Sound-hole circle and into the board underneath. This is to accommodate the central bolt of your circle-cutter.

7   Make sure that the blade in your cutter is very sharp. Wedge it in position with its flat surface inwards (towards the centre bolt), and projecting 1mm below the tool-bar. This will give a perpendicular cut of the right depth for the inner edge of the Rosette groove.

8   Adjust the length of the tool-bar so that the point of the cutter enters your knife-mark at the inner edge of the Rosette, and clamp the bar tightly in this position with its wedge.

9   Check carefully that everything is in order before making the first light cut. Don't attempt to go to the full depth of 1mm in one revolution of the cutter.

10   When the lower face of the tool-bar is rubbing on the Sound-board, remove the bar and re-set the cutter for the outer circle. This time, the flat face must be outwards (away from the centre bolt). Check with the Rosette, that the new setting of the tool-bar is perfectly accurate.

11   Cut the outer circle (15.1), noting that the tool must be turned in the opposite direction due to the changed angle of the cutting edge, and then remove the circle-cutter.

15.1 **Cutting the edges of the groove**

12   Pare away the waste between the two cuts to a depth of 1mm with a razor-sharp chisel (15.2). Work very slowly, paring off small, thin shavings so that you will not slip outside the ring. You may find it helpful to make an angled cut around the edges of the groove first, and then clear the centre portion. When you have reached the required depth, smooth the bottom of the groove, using the chisel like a scraper (15.3).

13   Try your Rosette in the groove. It should be an easy press-fit. If it is too tight, take a paring off the outside edge of the groove with the cutter; if too slack, you can fill the gap later by rubbing in a mixture of fine saw-dust and P.V.A. glue. (Matching saw-dust must be used, obtained by rubbing an off-cut of spruce on sandpaper.) As a last resort, a wider Rosette ring can be fitted.

14   Apply P.V.A. to the groove and position the Rosette so that its join comes near the top where it will be hidden under the Finger-board (15.4). The pattern at the bottom should be placed symmetrically in relation to the Sound-board joint.

15   Press in the Rosette and wipe away the excess glue with a clean damp cloth. It can be tapped gently home with a hammer and a wooden block if necessary. If you feel that pressure is needed, use a small flat board with a heavy weight on top (not forgetting the grease-proof paper!).

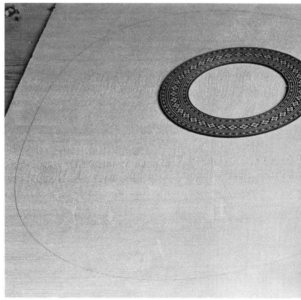

16   In about an hour the glue will have hardened sufficiently to commence the pleasurable task of levelling off the inlay. Using a very sharp smoothing plane or block plane, take it down almost flush with the spruce. Scrape away the remainder with a cabinet scraper. This will give a smooth, clean surface. Avoid sandpapering because this forces coloured wood dust into the grain of the spruce, and it can be difficult, if not

impossible, to remove.

Take great care not to damage the face of your Sound-board. Keep the surface clear of shavings so that they will not get trapped under the plane.

Making your own Rosette

Rosettes can be made individually, or several at a time. When examined closely, they resemble a mosaic, but in fact, the name given to this type of work is Tunbridge-ware, because it originated in England at Tunbridge Wells, Kent, in the 19th century. The pattern is created by gluing together strips of coloured veneer about 1mm thick, and cutting this multi-coloured sandwich lengthwise into slices 1mm thick. This process is repeated many times, placing the veneers in a different order for each sandwich according to the pattern being formed. One slice from each is then selected, and these are all glued together in a set sequence to form what is called a 'log'. By cutting this 'log' cross-wise into 1mm slices, a large number of little 'tiles' are produced which conform to the original design. In some designs, they are made up from the end grain of hundreds of 1mm square strips of veneer (15.5). If a single Rosette is being made, it can either be built up around a circle of

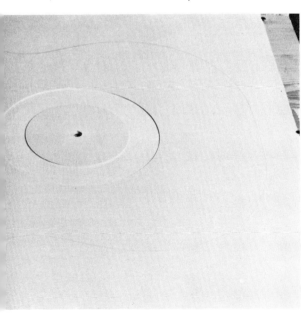

hardboard to produce a ring, or the complete Rosette can be assembled directly in the groove cut in the Sound-board. Depending on the pattern, several long, narrow strips of veneer are bent and glued in first, then the 'tiles' are fitted around and glued, followed by more long strips.

Mass-produced Rosettes are made on a former resembling a large tube. It has an outside diameter

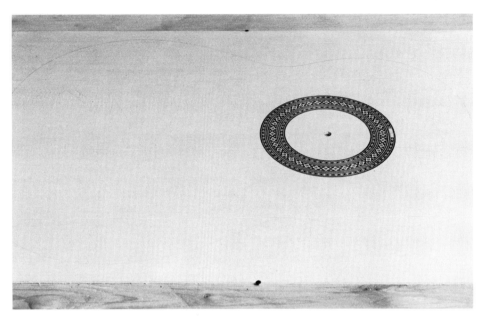

15.4 **The Rosette ring glued in place**

equal to the inside diameter of the Rosette ring, i.e. 4mm larger than the Sound-hole. Quite large sheets of veneer are wrapped around it and glued, followed by a complete layer of 'logs', fitted and glued side by side around the former. More sheets of veneer are glued round on top, and then the whole assembly is cramped tightly in a circular metal collar until the glue is dry. After the former has been pulled out, complete Rosette rings can be cut off as required, like slicing rashers of bacon.

Plan your pattern very carefully on graph paper. Coloured inks can be used to reproduce your design exactly. The squares are then numbered so that the plan can be followed easily when making up your layers of veneer. The Rosettes made by the masters of the art are fantastically complicated, but it would be wise to use a fairly simple geometric design for your first attempt.

15.5 **A Rosette 'tile' cut from the 'log'**

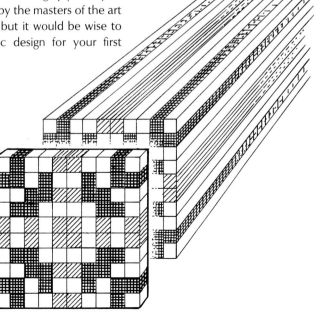

16 THICKNESSING, CUTTING OUT THE SOUND-HOLE, AND FAN STRUTTING

Before the task of strutting can commence, your Sound-board must be reduced in thickness to 2–2½mm. This is quite a delicate procedure, but vital in the construction of a fine classical guitar. If the board is too thick it will be rigid, and the response will be poor. On the other hand, over-thinning results in too much movement and produces unwanted overtones. This over-sensitivity can be controlled to a large extent by the system of strutting glued underneath, so it is better to err on the side of thinness, with 2mm as the minimum.

No hard and fast rules exist and every maker has his own pet theory about what the final thickness should be. A lot depends on the feel of the wood. Some pieces of spruce are stiffer than others and demand more thinning to achieve the necessary flexibility. Flex the board gently in your hands as you reduce it below the 2½mm level, and you may find that something seems to tell you, 'Stop, that's enough!' This is the realm where the guitar-maker becomes a creative artist, and he has only intuition and sensitivity to guide him.

When you are in the early stages of thicknessing, try to work systematically. I will assume that you are using the home-made pencil caliper described in Chapter 4, but the instructions still apply if you own a clock caliper.

1   16.1 shows a Sound-board being thicknessed. It is clamped securely face down to the work-board with a stiff batten, but be sure to check the surface of your work-bench and clean off any saw-dust or glue spots to prevent your carefully prepared face from being dented. A very low-set bench-stop is also shown in the illustration—it provides added security.

2   Thicknessing is best done in stages, so set your caliper to a gap of 2½mm for the first step.

16.1 **Thicknessing the Sound-board**

16.2 **Checking the thickness with a pencil caliper**

3 Plane a strip of the board along the edge, about the width of the plane, releasing the board and testing with the caliper until the pencil just moves over the surface without making a mark (16.2). Thicker areas will show themselves up very clearly.

4 Work across the board in strips like this until you have planed it down to 2½mm all over.

5 Now, using a well prepared cabinet scraper (see Chapter 3), reduce your Sound-board still further until it has a thickness of from 2–2½mm (16.3).

6 Set your circle cutter to a radius of 42mm and prepare to cut out the Sound-hole. Use the same drilled board you prepared for the Rosette inlaying. Make your first light cut with the blade protruding about 2½mm (vertical cutting-face outwards), and proceed in stages until the circle of spruce comes away (16.4). Do not round the edge of the hole; this will be done after gluing on the Finger-board.

16.3 **Scraping the Sound-board to its final thickness**

16.4 **Cutting out the Sound-hole**

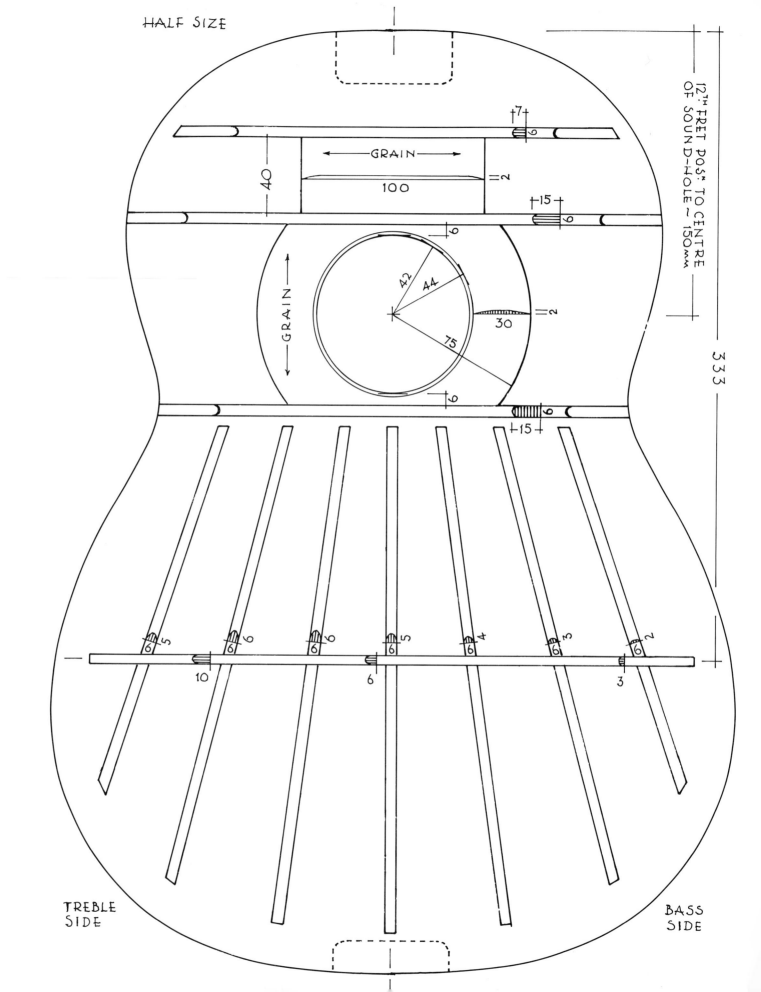

HALF SIZE

12ᵀᴴ FRET POSⁿ TO CENTRE OF SOUND-HOLE ~ 150ᴍᴍ

333

GRAIN

100

40

7

6

15

6

6

GRAIN

42

44

75

30

2

6

6

15

6

5

6

6

6

6

6

5

4

3

2

6

6

6

6

6

6

6

10

6

3

16.5

TREBLE SIDE

BASS SIDE

Strutting

Three types of strutting are employed under the Sound-board. The Sound-hole edge stiffening is glued first, then the fan-strutting, followed by the main supporting bars. These larger bracings are glued last so that the thinner struts and stiffeners can be shaped more easily with a plane and chisel. The layout of the bracing system, the number of struts used and the dimensions of individual struts, is extremely variable, and, as with thicknessing, all makers have their own ideas on the subject. For your first instrument, however, I recommend that you follow the design and dimensions shown in 16.5. It is based on the Torres pattern, but with small changes in the sectional dimensions of the fan-struts. These changes are necessary for the modern, larger-bodied guitar. Robert Bouchet, a well known French luthier who has produced many outstanding instruments, has experimented a great deal with strutting systems, and he finds that the addition of a Bridge Bar helps to even up the tonal balance between bass and treble. Recent scientific investigations into the behaviour of resonating Sound-boards have confirmed his ideas fairly conclusively. Several experienced luthiers have adopted the principle, but the dimensions of their bars vary considerably, from José Romanillos's thin plate to Robert Bouchet's deep-sectioned bar. However, the addition of a Bridge Bar complicates the construction slightly and if you would rather not use it on your first guitar, ignore instruction No. 21 and any other references in the text. The struts across the base of the Sound-board in the Torres system are considered by some luthiers to be unnecessary.

7   Cut out the Sound-board with a coping-saw or fret-saw. Allow about 5mm outside the line for final trimming (16.6).

8   Remove the wedges and inner mould sections, and gently ease the guitar from the mould, taking care not to strain the Neck joint.

9   Trim the top edge of the Sound-board to fit snugly against the 2mm step on the Neck, with the Sides lined up on the centre-joint. Check (from the plan) that the Sound-hole is in the correct position in relation to the Neck/Sides joint, and adjust the height of the Top Block so that the face of the Sound-board lies flush with the Neck surface.

10   Turn the assembly over and rest a weight on the Sides whilst you draw round the exterior outline, also around the interior Linings and Blocks.

11   Replace your guitar in the mould so that it retains its shape, and clamp the Sound-board face down to the

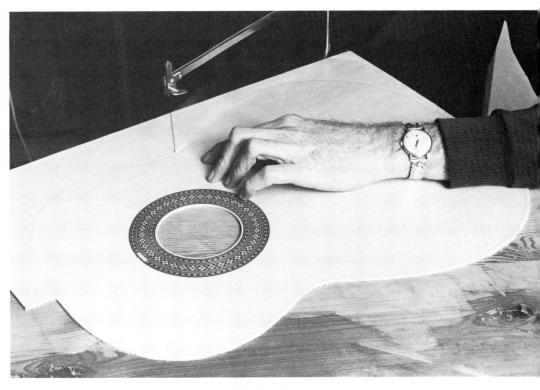

16.6 **Cutting out the Sound-board**

clean, guitar-shaped work-board, using blocks of softwood under the cramps. Mark the position of all the struts and bars with a soft pencil. Use a set-square lined up on the centre-joint to draw the cross-bracings.

12   Prepare all the struts, bars and stiffenings to the dimensions and grain directions shown on the plan. Ideally, the spruce for all the bars and struts should be cleft rather than sawn, so that the grain fibres run through the full length of each piece. Vibrations run along these fibres, spreading their effects across the whole Sound-board. Use a marking gauge and try-square, and plane all the faces and edges flat and square with each other, working from one true face. Make all the fan-struts 6 × 6mm. The final shaping to the required sections can be done more easily after they have been glued on.

13   Glue the Sound-hole stiffening with Cascamite, clamping it down by placing a wood-block on top to spread the pressure of the cramp.

14   Prepare a long, slightly concave clamping batten. This will provide extra pressure at the ends of the struts.

15   Glue all the fan-struts in place one by one, leaving them clamped down for about half-an-hour. I like to use P.V.A. glue for these, not only because the gluing operation can be completed in a few hours, but also because the film of glue in the joint is more flexible than Cascamite would be, and flexibility combined with

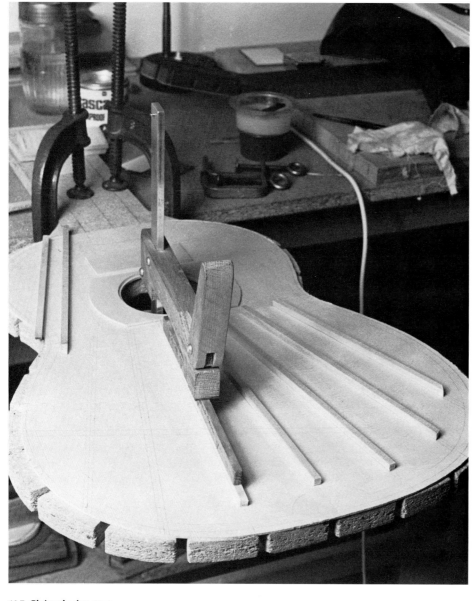

strength is what we are aiming for. Note that their ends do not touch other bars or blocks. *16.7* shows the fan-strutting being glued and clamped. This is where your guitar-maker's cramps will be most useful. (See Chapter 4.)

16   After the glue has set, inspect all the struts very closely to make certain that they are securely fixed to the Sound-board. Poorly glued strutting can cause buzzing noises and bad tone.

17   Shape the stiffening and the struts to the sections shown on the plan with a block-plane and chisel, all the ends being carefully tapered down to the surface of the Sound-board. This is where cleft wood has a further advantage; it will cut with equal ease in either direction when using a chisel. Note carefully that the struts are not of uniform section right across the Sound-board. They become progressively thinner towards the outer edges, especially on the bass side (the right-hand side as you work). The thicker bracing on the treble side is necessary to control the higher frequencies. To protect the Sound-board from damage during this operation, thin strips of metal or plastic can be taped at either side of the strut you are working on. I am using ½mm zinc in the photograph (*16.8*).

18   Chamfer the edges of the Sound-hole stiffening with a very sharp chisel to form a gently rounded shape, especially on the inner edges, so that they will not be visible through the Sound-hole from the front of the guitar.

19   The main cross-bracing bars above and below the Sound-hole must now have their gluing surfaces gently curved (*16.9*). This will give a slight fullness to the body, and also create a very small amount of tension in the Sound-board. It is believed that this improves the tone of the guitar.

16.7 Gluing the fan-struts

16.9 The curved Sound-board bars

HALF SIZE

SECTION A-A
FULL SIZE

15

6

BAR 1 (UPPER BOUT)

1 MM   1 MM

BAR 2 (WAIST)

2 MM   2 MM

A

A

16.8 **Shaping the fan-struts**

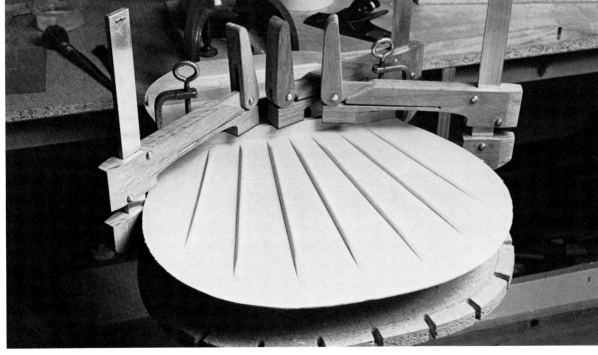

16.10 **Cramping the bars**

20 Glue the cross-bracings with Cascamite, clamping them to the Sound-board using a set-up similar to the one shown in *16.10*. It is good practice to clamp up dry

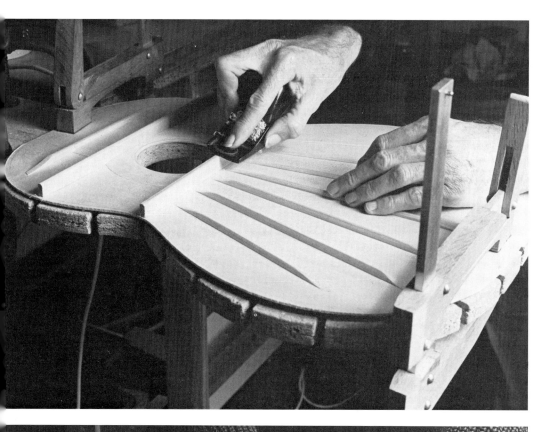

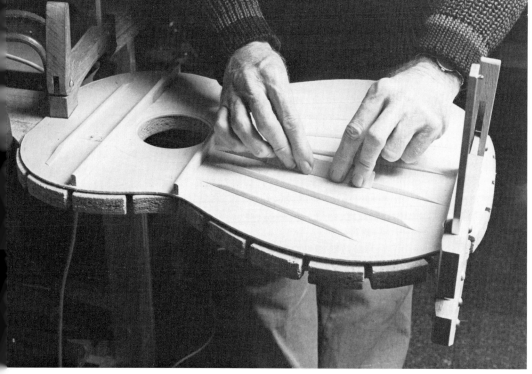

initially to make certain that the gluing surfaces are in perfect contact. After the glue has set, shape their tops to the half-round sections shown on the plan with a block-plane and sanding-block. Do not scallop the ends at this stage (16.11). Smooth the fan-struts with a strip of sandpaper (16.12).

21 The Bridge Bar must be glued exactly beneath the position where the ivory Bridge Saddle will eventually be fitted on the Bridge. Mark this point on the underside

16.11 **Shaping the tops of the bars**

16.12 **Smoothing the fan-struts**

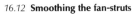

16.13 **Marking the position of the Bridge Bar**

of your Sound-board in the following manner. Place the board face downwards on the Sides. Then, with a long batten marked accurately with the scale-length of 66cm and the half-scale length of 33cm, set the 33cm mark exactly over the point where the Sides join the Neck. This will be the important 12th fret position. The top mark should come 5mm down the Neck from the lower edge of the Head facing, indicating the upper end of the Finger-board. This gap will hold the 5mm wide ivory Nut. The 66cm mark is the uncompensated position of the inner (closest to the Sound-hole) edge of the 2mm thick ivory Saddle. (Compensation will be explained in Chapter 24.) Now draw a line across the underside of the Sound-board 3mm below this 66cm mark, at a right-angle to the centre-line. This position, 66.3cm from the Nut, represents the compensated scale-length, plus 1mm, which is half the thickness of the Bridge Saddle (16.13).

The gluing surface of the 10mm × 5mm Bridge Bar must be given a slight curve. Plane and smooth it until it fits into the curve of No. 3 Back Bar clamping batten (see Chapter 4), then locate your Bridge Bar exactly over the position-line and mark both sides of the Bar to indicate where small slots must be cut to fit over each fan strut. Fit the Bar very carefully before gluing, and just to make certain that it rests on the Sound-board at all points, place a piece of tissue paper (e.g. cigarette paper) in the joint; the paper must be gripped by the Bar. Set up the cramping arrangement carefully before applying the glue, positioning the No. 3 batten beneath the Sound-board (16.14). The clamps should press the Sound-board down evenly into the curve. Glue the Bar in place with Cascamite, and when it has set, taper it as shown in 16.15, rounding its top edge smoothly.

22   Smooth the struts, bars and stiffenings with a small piece of the finest sandpaper, rounding off all the sharp edges. A carefully finished interior is one of the signs of a well made guitar; it also results in a more efficient sound chamber.

16.14 **Gluing the Bridge Bar in place**

16.15 **The shaped Bridge Bar and Bridge clamping block**

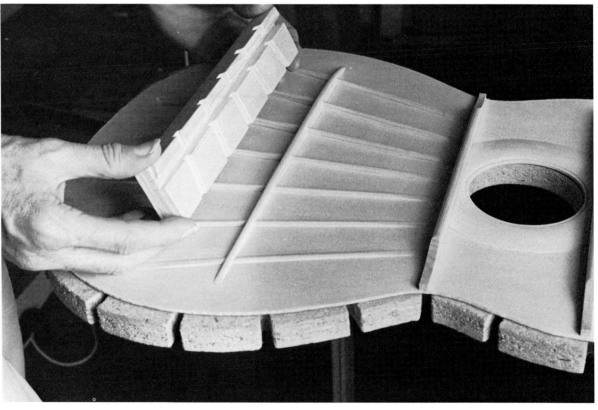

Make the Bridge clamping block described in Chapter 4 before you store your finished Sound-board away in a safe place until the time comes to glue it in position on the Sides.

17 PREPARING THE BACK AND INLAYING THE BOTTOM JOINT

Preparing the Back

The wood for the Back is prepared in the same way as the spruce Sound-board, so instructions 1–10 in Chapter 14 will apply, followed by the jointing suggestions. Match the grain of your two halves where they join, and if you are using rosewood, the grain configurations should curve in towards the centre at the top and bottom of the Back, with the widest curve coming in the lower bout (17.1).

The centre joint is usually covered with an inlay of decorative wood. Although most top quality guitars have this feature, it serves no practical purpose. A maple Back, with its characteristic flamed figuring, has a very handsome appearance without this extra adorn-ment, provided that the joint is well made. Purfling strips can be inlaid around the edges of the Back, and at each side of the centre strip, all the corners being carefully mitred (see Chapter 20). These decorations involve many hours of meticulous work, and as the only compulsory addition to the Back is the protective Edging strip, you must decide for yourself how much time and effort you wish to devote to them.

If you intend to include a centre strip on your guitar, sufficient material for this purpose can be salvaged from the edges of the Back before it is thicknessed and cut to shape. Purfling strips can be glued at each side of the centre strip before inlaying it over the joint. Choose black/white/black or white/black/white purfling to contrast with a maple or a rosewood Back.

1   Prepare a strip of rosewood 51cm × 3mm × 1½mm as in 17.2.

2   Prepare two clamping battens 55cm × 2½cm × 8mm.

3   Nail one batten to a flat work-board with panel-pins.

4   Protect the edges of both battens, and the board surface, with Scotch tape.

5   Apply P.V.A. glue to the appropriate edges of the rosewood and purfling strips.

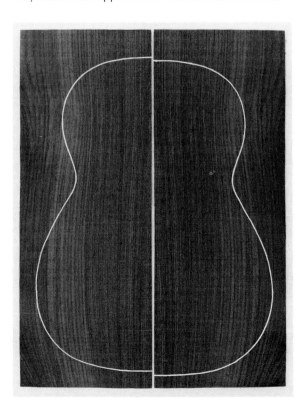

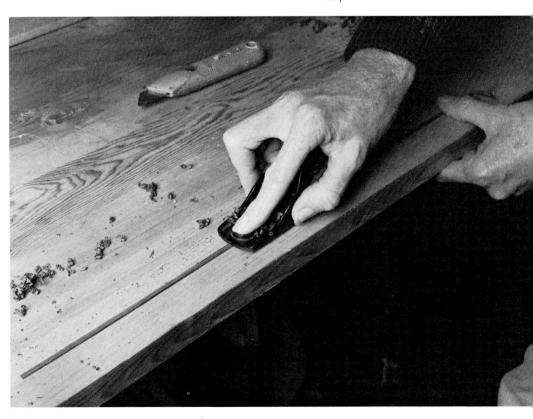

17.1 The grain formation of a rosewood Back

17.2 Preparing a strip of rosewood inlay

6 Press all the strips together with the other batten and nail it down until the glue has hardened (17.3). Make certain that they are all pressed down to the work-board.

7 Smooth the under-surface of your inlay with a block-plane.

8 Place it in position over the centre joint and mark its exact width on the Back with a Stanley knife.

9 Clamp down a steel straight-edge set to the marks, and make a shallow knife-cut.

10 Move the straight-edge to the other side and make another cut.

11 With a chisel which is narrower than your desired

17.3 **Gluing together the decorative strips for the Back**

groove, scrape the waste wood away between the knife-cuts, using the clamped straight-edge as a guide for the chisel. If you burr the edge of the chisel it will work like a cabinet scraper.

12 Move the straight-edge to the other side and scrape again.

13 Remove the straight-edge and check the depth of the groove, which should not be deeper than one millimetre. Keep moving the straight-edge from side to side, scraping out the groove until you have achieved the required depth.

14 When the inlay is a push-fit in the groove, glue it in place with P.V.A., pressing it well down with the head of a hammer.

15 Wipe away the glue and place a flat, heavy weight on top.

16 When the glue is dry, scrape the inlay down level with the surface of the Back.

The Back is thicknessed from the reverse side to 2–2 ½mm (17.4 and 17.5) using the method set out in Chapter 16. Some luthiers 'tune' the Back to the Sound-board by tapping with the knuckles, listening to the resonating note and removing a little more wood until the desired tone is reached. There is no set formula which can be employed—it's all a matter of intuition combined with long experience—but the Back vibrations should fall within the same frequency range as the Sound-board so that they are in partnership rather than fighting with one another. Hold the board up vertically between finger and thumb, and strike it sharply near the bottom with a finger-knuckle of the other hand. As you thin the board down, you will notice that the resonating note gradually becomes lower.

17.4 **A jointed rosewood Back being thicknessed**

17.5 **Finishing with a cabinet scraper**

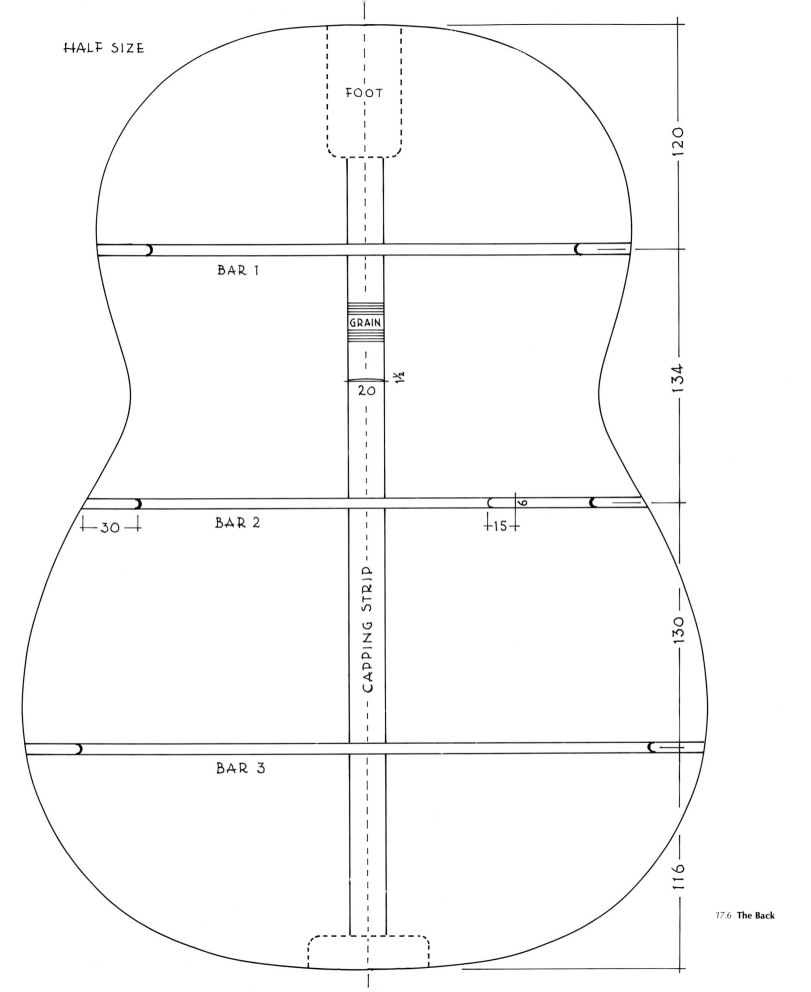

HALF SIZE

FOOT

120

BAR 1

GRAIN

134

20   1½

BAR 2

6

30   15

CAPPING STRIP

130

BAR 3

116

17.6 **The Back**

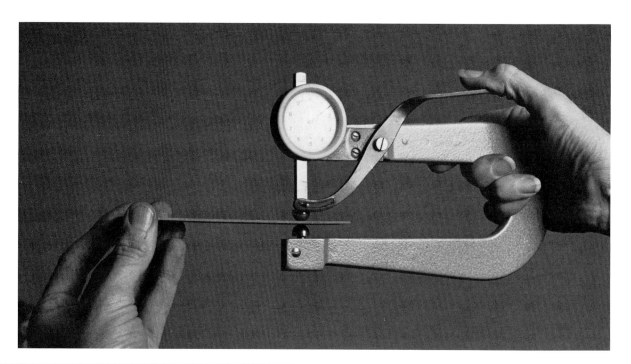

17.7 **A section of cross-grained capping strip being measured**

17.8 **Rounding off the capping strip**

from mahogany, but with the grain running across its width; this provides the maximum reinforcement for the Back joint. It butts up against the Foot and Bottom Block, so allow a few millimetres extra in length for fitting after it has been glued in place. As it is almost impossible to make a cross-grained strip as long and thin as this without breakage, shorter pieces can be butted together. Arrange for the joins to come where the Back bars will be fitted, so indicate their positions on the centre-line. (Note from the diagram (*17.6*) that they are not quite equidistant). *17.7* shows a section of capping being measured with a dial caliper.

4 Glue the capping, a section at a time, with P.V.A. between previously drawn guide-lines, pressing them in place with your fingers until they no longer have a tendency to slide. Wipe away the squeezed-out glue, and place a heavy weight on top (your fore-plane resting on a flat batten, for instance).

5 Round off the top of the strip, first with a very sharp chisel as in *17.8*, then with sandpaper. The edges are not cut right down to a feather-edge because they would tend to become ragged. Remember that this capping strip will be visible through the Sound-hole so a clean appearance is essential.

With a final thickness of 2–2½mm, the note sounded is usually around 'A' or 'G'. All tuning of this kind should be done before the bars are glued on.

The capping strip

1 Mark out the Back shape with your template and cut it with a coping-saw or fret-saw, allowing a few millimetres outside the line.

2 Scrape the wood to a satin smooth finish.

3 Prepare a capping strip to glue over the centre joint. As you will see from the illustrations, the strip is made

Fitting the bars

The Back of a classical guitar is slightly domed. As mentioned in Chapter 1, the resulting concave surface inside the instrument helps to project the sound

74

forwards through the Sound-hole. The internal volume of the body is increased without affecting the overall size of the instrument, and the Back itself is strengthened by the curvature. Being under slight tension, it is also less liable to 'flutter'.

Three bars are used to support the Back and provide the domed shape. They are usually made from mahogany or cedar for a rosewood Back, or spruce for a maple Back. Their preparation is similar to that described for the main bars of the Sound-board, and their dimensions are given on the drawing (17.6). Although not quite as important as the Sound-board bars, they must, nevertheless, be made with care from straight-grained wood. Allow 2cm or so to spare on the length of each bar for fitting purposes.

Gluing these shaped bars in place on the Back can present problems, and the desired curvature of the Back will not be achieved unless some preparation work is done. The simple, direct cramping arrangement used for the Sound-board is not sufficient for the Back, which is less flexible, and more deeply arched in the waist area. Some makers clamp the Back into a specially hollowed out work-board, but the time involved in scooping out an accurate concave shape of this size could only be justified if you intend to make several guitars. Don't be tempted to rely on springy battens underneath the Back to pull it up to the bars; I tried this method once, and the result was a flat Back and bent bars!

The answer to the problem is to use the three hollowed-out clamping battens, one for each bar, as described in Chapter 4. The gluing surfaces of the bars are curved like those for the Sound-board, the varying amounts of curvature being taken from their individual clamping battens.

1   Shape the bars with a spokeshave and sanding stick, checking that the edges are square with the sides.

2   Fit them into the curve of the batten by sighting against the light. This will show up any irregularities.

3   Number the bars 1, 2, 3, to match their battens.

4   Mark the outlines of the bars on the Back with a set-square, and cut notches in the capping strip to receive them (17.9).

5   Set up your clamping arrangement (17.10), and clamp the bars in place dry to make absolutely certain that they are in close contact right across the Back. A slight change in the position of a cramp will often cure a minor gap.

6   Glue each bar in separately with Cascamite, leaving it to set thoroughly before moving on to the next.

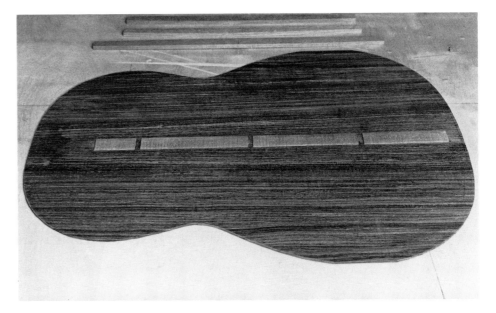

17.9 **The capping strip notched for the Back bars**

17.10 **Gluing the bars**

Inlaying the Bottom Joint

The butted joint of the Sides on the Bottom Block must now be hidden behind an inlaid strip like the centre joint of the Back. Make up a short length of identical inlay allowing a centimetre or so over in length for fitting. Follow the same procedure as before when making the groove, clamping your guitar in the vice by its Bottom Block (17.11). As will be seen from the photograph, a lot of ingenuity is required in the art of guitar making. After gluing (17.12), the strip is cut to length and scraped down flush with the Sides.

17.11 **The groove for the Bottom Joint inlay**

17.12 **The inlay ready to be levelled**

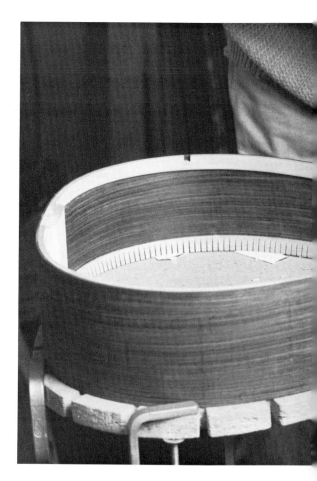

18 FITTING THE BACK

Fitting is a very demanding procedure, and it is only by constant checking and correcting that a perfectly glued Back can be achieved. Never hesitate to take everything apart during fitting to enable small adjustments to be made.

1   Secure the Back to the work-board with your guitar-maker's cramps, inserting some packing around the edges to take up the curvature, and to avoid straining it in any way.

2   Round off the tops of the bars with block-plane and sandpaper.

3   Scallop the ends of the bars to the dimensions given. Do this with a broad chisel, working with the angled face of the tool against the wood (18.1).

4   The ends of the bars are let into notches cut in the Linings, and to find their positions, rest the Back on the Sides. Line it up accurately with the centre of the Heel and the bottom inlay, holding the assembly in place on the work-board with rubber bands stretched across the Back. Make certain that the Neck is in true alignment.

5   Mark the Linings where the bars cross them with a very sharp pencil; also mark the bars where they cross the outside face of the Sides.

6   Remove the Back and draw another line across the ends of the bars, parallel to the first line and 2mm inwards of it. This compensates for the thickness of the Sides. Cut off the waste ends on this second line.

7   Mark the depth of the notches on the inside of the Linings with a pair of compasses set to 5mm.

8   Draw perpendicular lines down the Linings to mark the sides of the notches, and cut them out with a small chisel (18.2). Two saw-cuts can be made initially at the sides of each notch. Note that the notches must never encroach further than the glue-line between the Sides and the Linings.

9   Place the Back on the Sides to try the fit. Some adjustment of the bar ends and notches will certainly be necessary.

18.1 **Scalloping the ends of the bars**

18.2 **Cutting the notches for the Back bars**

10   Turn the guitar over with the Back held firmly in place, and mark the ends of the centre capping strip where they will butt up against the Foot and Bottom Block.

11   Cut off the waste with a chisel.

12   Due to the arch of the Back, the Sides and Linings must now be lowered slightly at the upper and lower bout positions to achieve a close fit all round. This is more easily done with the Sides held in the mould (one layer must be unscrewed). Work slowly with block-plane and sanding-stick, being careful not to remove too much wood. Keep testing the fit of the Back, and chiselling a shaving off the scalloped ends of the bars so that they press right down into the notches.

13   When you have achieved a close fit all round, give the gluing surfaces a slight angle so that they will make close contact with the domed Back.

14   The Foot and Bottom Block will also need attention—the angle of the gluing surfaces will almost certainly have to be changed. Do this with a broad paring chisel and sanding-stick, giving the final surfaces a slight roundness to fit the curvature of the Back.

The base of the Heel is pared down flush with the Sides and Linings, and will later be capped with a piece of rosewood or ebony to bring it up to the level of the Back.

15   When you are completely satisfied with the fit of the Back, clamp your guitar to the work-board by its Neck with packing under the Sides where necessary.

16   Check that the centre-lines register perfectly, and make sure that you have plenty of strong rubber bands large enough to stretch across the guitar in all directions.

17   Apply Cascamite to the surfaces where the Back will come in contact—the Sides and Linings, Foot and Bottom Block, not forgetting the six notches.

18   Place the Back on carefully and hold it down with a few bands whilst you make a final check that everything is in order. A clamp can be put on lightly over the Bottom Block to hold the assembly in place on the centre-line.

19   Stretch bands across the Back in all directions, pulling down the edges firmly all round, until every part is held in close contact with the Sides (18.3). You should be able to see some glue squeezing out of the joint; this will be removed later when the overlapping edges are pared down flush with the Sides. Some glue will also have been squeezed out on the inside of the joint. This

18.3 **Gluing on the Back**

78

will be scraped away before gluing on the Sound-board.

After about six hours, the overlapping edges can be pared off (18.4), your guitar can be turned over and the inside cleaned up in readiness for sealing with two coats of varnish. See 18.5 and Chapter 25. I recommend this treatment of the inside for the following reasons: the varnish helps to protect the wood from sudden humidity changes, and it also assists in the removal of moisture-collecting dust, which can be done when the strings are being renewed, but perhaps the greatest advantage of varnishing the interior is that the dust-free, shiny surface improves the sound reflecting properties of the domed Back.

The underside of the Sound-board is left untreated, so you are now ready to tackle the fitting and gluing on of this vital component.

18.4 **Paring off the overlap**

18.5 **Varnishing the interior**

19 FITTING THE SOUND-BOARD

This is a very exciting moment. With the gluing of the Sound-board your guitar really begins to take shape; it resonates when you tap it, and you can almost hear the sonorous tones it will produce once the strings are on.

1 Secure your guitar to the work-board by fixing a cramp on the Neck with packing under the Heel, so that the body is resting on the centre of the Back. Insert small pieces of soft packing (cork or cardboard) in the gap under the Sides for support.

2 Place blocks under the Neck. The top face must be level with the Bottom Block. Test this Neck setting with a long straight-edge, and adjust the height of the blocks under the Neck until the exact angle is achieved (19.1). A slight lift to the Finger-board is created by gluing the Sound-board on top of the Bottom Block but recessing it into the Neck.

3 Scallop the two main bars as you did for the Back, so that their ends are 5mm in depth.

19.1 **Testing the angle of the Neck**

4 The ends of the bars are again notched into the Linings. Place the Sound-board in position on the Sides, lining up the centre joint with the centre-line on the Neck, and the centre of the inlay at the bottom. Align the top edge of the Sound-board (the half-scale mark) with the rebate you cut on the face of the Neck; a small set-square can be set up on the Neck to fix its position until the bars fit into their notches, and the Sound-board can come in contact with the Sides.

5 Mark the ends of the bars where they cross the Sides, at the same time marking the Linings where the bars cross them.

6 Remove the Sound-board and draw another line on the bars as you did when fitting the Back, to indicate the inside face of the Sides.

7 Cut off the ends of the bars (19.2).

8 Cut the notches in the Linings to a depth of 5mm to receive the ends of the bars (19.3).

9 Test the fit of the Sound-board (19.4). The important thing to check is that the notches are deep enough to allow the board to come into close contact with the

19.2 **Shortening the main bracing bars to fit into the Linings**

Sides and Linings. Plane down the Sides and Linings gradually as you did when fitting the Back, re-scalloping the ends of the bars as you proceed, until your Sound-board lies in perfect contact all round. The Sides will not require to be lowered quite as much as when fitting the

19.3 **Cutting the notches in the Linings**

19.4 **Trying the fit of the Sound-board**

19.6 **Gluing on the Sound-board**

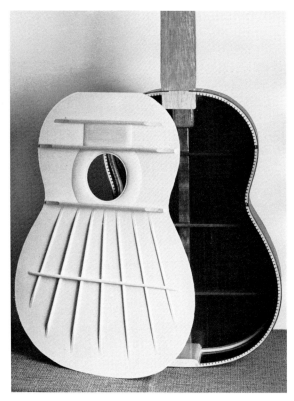

19.5 **The Sound-board ready for gluing to the Sides**

19.7 **Smoothing the edges at the waist**

Back because the Sound-board is flatter.

10   Make quite certain that the Top and Bottom Blocks are exactly the right height; a high Bottom Block will cause an unsightly bump on the Sound-board, and a low Block, of course, will result in a dent. Watch that the ends of the bars in their notches are not forcing the Sides apart.

11   Smooth the tops of the Sides and Linings with a sanding-stick. Due to the flexibility of the spruce, you will have to make allowances whilst fitting, pressing the board down on to the Sides in places.

12   When you are completely satisfied that no further adjustments are required, run a pencil around the edges to mark the final position, which may vary a fraction from your original outline.

13   Remove the Sound-board and pare off the excess to within about 2mm of the new line. This is very important because otherwise the downward pull of the rubber bands on the overhanging edges will distort your Sound-board, or even break the edges off, especially at the bouts. *19.5* shows the completed Sound-board ready for gluing.

14   Spread a thin, even coat of Cascamite on the Sides and Linings, both Blocks, and the notches for the bars. Press your Sound-board into place and hold it down tightly with plenty of rubber bands in the same way as when gluing the Back (*19.6*). Cramps can be applied very lightly over the Top and Bottom Blocks.

After allowing at least 6 hours for the glue to set, remove all the rubber bands. Then, working with the grain, gently pare off all the overlapping edges with a block plane and sanding-sticks as in *19.7*. This is one of the most enjoyable tasks in the whole operation.

Slight distortion of the body shape usually takes place with the gluing of the Back and Sound-board. This is nothing to worry about. If you have been careful to register up all the centre-lines, any small discrepancies will be symmetrical.

20   EDGING AND PURFLING

The Edgings and Purflings on a guitar have some important practical functions quite apart from their decorative value. They seal the grain at the edges of the Sound-board and Back, and the Edgings (sometimes called bindings), being made from hardwood, protect the instrument against knocks and hard usage. The edges of very old guitars were often elaborately inlaid but tastes have changed, and makers of classical guitars since Torres have been content with a less ornate and, to my mind, more elegant appearance.

I will describe two methods. The first is a simplified version for newcomers to instrument-making. The second is for your next guitar or for more advanced craftsmen, and, except for the type of glue, is the method used by the well-known French luthier, Robert Bouchet, to whom I am indebted for his helpful advice.

A rebate has to be cut around the edges of the guitar. The Edgings, which can be of a contrasting wood to enhance the colour of your Back and Sides, are then bent on the bending iron and glued in place. Start with the Back.

METHOD 1 (20.1)

1   Prepare your four Edging strips by planing two adjacent sides flat and square. Do this by clamping the strips to the bench by one end, and planing away from the cramp as you did when preparing the Linings. All four strips can be placed side by side and planed together.

2   Clamp your guitar face down to the work-board, with cramps at the Neck and over the Bottom Block. Remember to protect the face of the Sound-board with some soft material (carpet off-cuts are useful for this), and to insert suitable pieces of packing under the Sides and the Neck.

3   Your purfling cutter must now be adjusted. First of all, make quite certain that the blade is razor-sharp. You may need to experiment a little here to discover the shape of cutting edge which suits you best. I prefer a

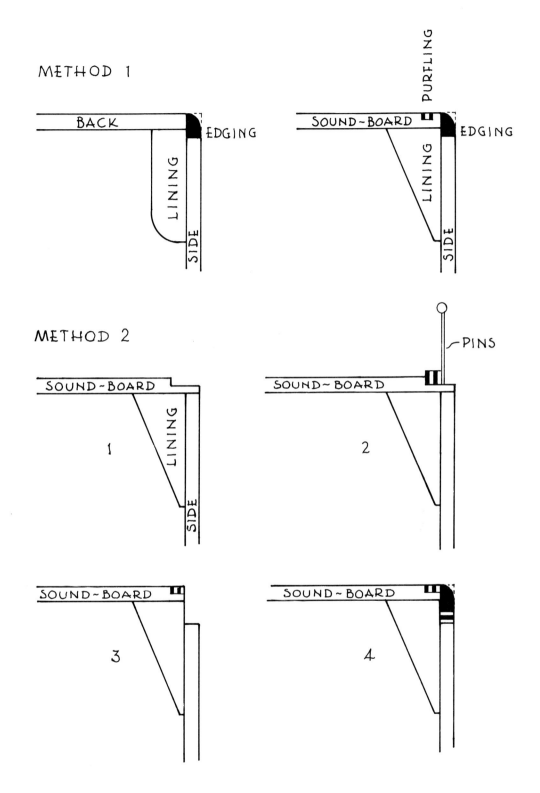

semi-circular shape. A pointed blade is always breaking, damaging the wood and sometimes leaving its point embedded in the cut, whereas a rounded blade

20.1

83

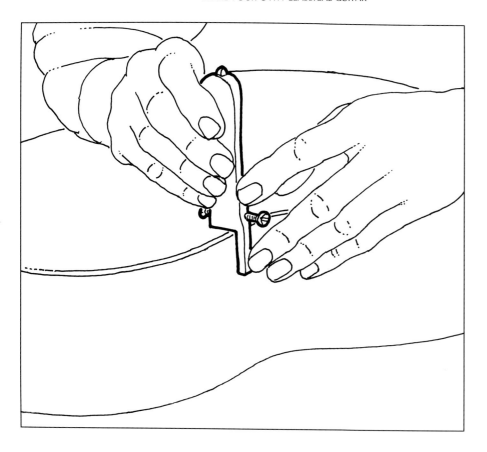

20.2 **Using a purfling cutter on the Back**

20.3 **Using the purfling cutter on the Sides**

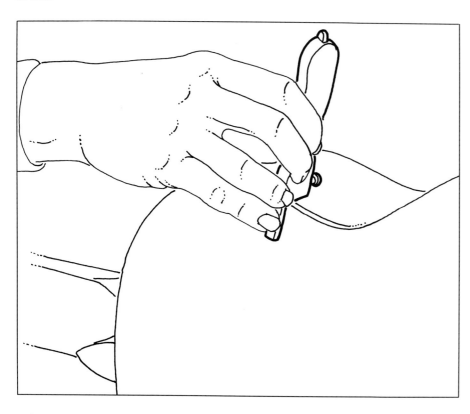

cuts through the grain cleanly rather than trying to follow it and wandering off course. With the flat side of the blade facing outwards to give a vertical cut around the edge of the Back, set the gap between the cutting edge and the guide to just under the thickness of your Edging strips. The blade should be projecting about 3mm.

4   Test for accuracy of adjustment on a piece of waste wood.

5   Grip the tool in both hands with the guide pressed firmly against the Side (20.2), and make your first light cut right around the edge of the Back. It is very important to keep the tool perfectly upright and running smoothly with even pressure.

6   When the base of the tool touches the surface of the Back, extend the blade a further millimetre. Proceed in this way until your cut is the correct depth, depending upon the width of your Edgings.

7   Unclamp your guitar, and rest it on edge on the work-board (20.3). Readjust the cutting blade to just under the width of your strips, and again projecting 3mm.

8   Cut the Sides in stages as before until the edge comes away. Clean up the rebate to receive the Edgings using a hand-file with a plain edge.

9   Chisel away the base of the Heel to take the Edgings where they butt together on the centre-line. The Heel Capping will be glued on later to bring the Heel flush with the Back.

10   Heat up your bending iron, and bend the two strips for the Back Edging so that they lie snugly in their rebates.

11   Secure them tightly all round with rubber bands across the Back, and cut the bottom ends to butt together perfectly on the centre-line. Some makers surround the edge of their work-board with round-headed screws to hold the bands (20.9). Leave the top ends overlapping; they will be cut and butted together more accurately at a later stage.

12   Coat the rebate with P.V.A. glue from the bottom centre-line to about half way round the Lower Bout on one side only, and press the appropriate strip into place with the cut end exactly on the centre-line. Wipe away excess glue and secure the strip tightly with plenty of rubber bands.

13   Apply more glue to the waist section, press in the strip, wipe away the glue and stretch more bands across the Back.

14   Glue the Edging into the Upper Bout rebate, secure with bands, and cut off the end with a chisel exactly on the centre-line. The end of the strip can be held in firm contact with the edge of the Back by tapping a small chart pin into the base of the Heel, pressing tightly against the strip.

15   Leave the glue to harden thoroughly, then remove the rubber bands. Clear the rebate of any hardened glue where the butt joints will come, and proceed with the other side in the same way, starting at the bottom joint as before. When you reach the Heel, cut the end to butt closely with the first Edging, and secure it with

another pin.

16   When the rubber bands have been removed, you will have the pleasurable task of sanding the Edgings flush with the Sides and Back.

The Sound-board Edging is fitted in the same way, the only difference coming at the Neck, where the ends of the strips are let into notches cut with a fine chisel before the gluing is begun. These ends are later covered by the Finger-board. Make the notches project about 10mm into the Neck (20.4).

20.4 **The ends of the strips are let into notches**

Purfling (method 1)
Before the Finger-board is glued on, you may wish to decorate the edges of your Sound-board with an inlay. The black/white/black strips must be let into a groove cut 1mm inside the Edging (20.1).

1   Sharpen your purfling cutter blade.

2   Adjust the gap to make a cut 1mm away from the Edging strip, with the flat side of the blade facing inwards towards the guide to give a vertical side to the groove, and projecting 1mm.

3   Make the cut with the tool absolutely vertical.

4   Readjust the blade to make a second cut the thickness of your Purfling strip inside the first cut. Some purfling cutters can be fitted with two blades which can be set (with spacers between them) to make two cuts, the width of the Purfling strip apart.

5   The waste between the cuts can be removed to the required depth of 1mm with a fine chisel made from a small file, ground and sharpened at one end. Test the fit in the groove before proceeding too far.

6   The ends at the bottom are butted together, but at the top they are continued for 10mm like the Edgings, to be concealed later by the Finger-board.

7   Bend the strips on the bending iron, and then run P.V.A. glue into the groove with a water-colour brush. Press in the Purfling strips carefully with the head of a small hammer. Wipe away squeezed-out glue with a damp cloth as you proceed.

8   Leave to dry, and then scrape the Purfling down flush with the face of your Sound-board.

METHOD 2 (20.1)
1   Assuming that your Back and Sides are of rosewood, cut four strips of rosewood, 75 to 80cm long, and about 5mm × 4mm (unplaned) in section. Plane two adjacent edges flat and square on each strip, reducing the dimensions to about 4mm × 2½mm. These will be the gluing surfaces. The finished dimensions will be 3½mm × 2mm after gluing and fairing off.

2   Secure your guitar face-downwards to the work-board with a cramp on the Neck and packing in the gap underneath. Protect the Sound-board with some soft material, and support the edges with pieces of packing all round.

3   Set your purfling cutter to a width of 3½mm (2mm Edging plus 1½mm Purfling inlay) with the flat side of the blade facing outwards to give a vertical cut to the rebate.

20.5 **Mitring the inlays at the corners**

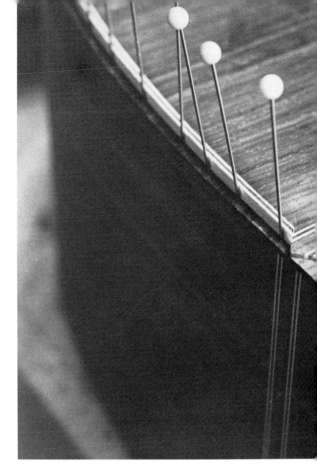

4   Make a light cut round the edge of the Back, *stopping well clear of the centre strip inlay.*

5   Deepen the cut gradually, and then make a shallow rebate with a very sharp chisel, bevelled side downwards.

6   Go round again with the cutter, then deepen the rebate until you reach a fairly even depth of about 1½mm. It is very important to ensure that the rebate has sharp, clean edges, and any attempt to smooth the sides with sandpaper usually results in rounding rather than flattening. A safe-edge file is the best tool to use for this.

7   At the centre strip, top and bottom, continue the rebate up to the edge of the inlay with a knife, steel rule, and chisel.

8   Cut a mitre in the inlay at both sides of the centre strip, top and bottom (20.5).

9   Bend two strips of white/black/white Purfling on the bending iron to fit accurately into the rebates.

10   Fit the inlay on one side temporarily with a few pins at the waist, and mitre the bottom end into the centre inlay.

11   Clean out any chippings, and apply P.V.A. with a small brush to about 10cm of rebate at the bottom. Position the mitred end, holding the strip in place with

20.6 **The Back Purfling glued and pinned**

20.7 **Cutting the Sides**

20.8 **Cutting the rebate**

pins (*20.5*).

12   Continue round one side to the top in 10cm stages using plenty of pins to hold the inlay tightly in the rebate.

13   Mitre the top end into the centre inlay with a very sharp knife, and hold with pins.

14   Scrape away surplus glue from the Back, and wipe with a damp cloth.

15   After half-an-hour or so, the pins can be removed and the other side completed (*20.6*).

16   Leave to harden thoroughly (two to three hours) before paring off the surplus inlay. A modified spokeshave is the ideal tool for this, if used with care. By masking off both ends of the blade with tape so that only the centre third is exposed, you will avoid digging into the Back. Finish off by scraping down level with the surface.

17   Re-sharpen and re-set your cutter to 5mm (3½mm Edging plus 1½mm inlay) for the Sides.

18   With your guitar resting securely on its side on some soft material, make a light cut, stopping short at the bottom inlay.

19   Deepen the cut (*20.7*), and then pare off the waste to form a rebate as you did on the Back (*20.8*). Extra care must be taken, however, because you are working with unpredictable grain on the bent Sides, and it is easy to splinter the wood. If this appears likely to happen, cut in the opposite direction. The rebate must be cut right down flush with the side of the Back Purfling, so that the rosewood Edging strip will fit closely against it.

20   Clean up the rebate using a small file with a plain edge, and bend your Edgings and white/black/white Purflings. When you are bending the rosewood strips, beware of twists. If you see a twist beginning, correct it on the iron before continuing with the bending, otherwise it will cause problems with fitting later on.

20.9 **Fitting the Back Edging and Side Purfling**

20.10 **Scarfing the Edgings at the bottom**

20.11 **Preparing the Heel Capping**

20.12 **Gluing the Heel Capping**

carefully jointed. One half of the scarf joint at the top can now be cut.

24   Starting at the bottom, glue the Edging strip and the Purfling inlay into the rebate, and to each other, a section at a time. Make certain that the mitring of the inlays fits perfectly, using plenty of rubber bands on the glued section before moving on.

25   Continue in this way to the top, bedding the strips into the rebate with finger pressure and stretching the bands across the Back. The strips can be held in place

21   Deal with one side of the guitar at a time. Fit the Edging and Purfling strips dry, holding them together in the rebate with a few rubber bands at the waist whilst you mitre the inlay at the bottom (20.9).

22   The joints between the two Edging strips can be butted on the centre-line, but a scarf joint is much stronger, and almost invisible. The scarf is positioned off-centre so that it will not be in the way when you mitre the inlays on the other side (20.10). Cut the scarf for one side only at this stage.

23   The base of the Heel must now be chiselled away to allow the Edging and Purfling to be continued around the top. The Heel Capping will eventually cover the ends of the Purfling inlay, but the Edging strips must be

on the Heel with a few pins.

26   When the glue has set, remove all the bands and deal with the other side. Cut and fit the scarf joint at the bottom after clearing out the old glue, and mitre the inlay (20.10).

27   Fit the strips in place dry, mark out and cut the top scarf, and butt joint the top ends of the inlay.

28   Glue in the strips.

29   Pare off the surplus, scraping down to a smooth finish on Sides and Back.

30   It is a good idea to fit the Heel Capping at this stage; the Back of the instrument will then be entirely finished and ready for varnishing. If your guitar is in rosewood, you will require a matching piece, 5mm thick, for the Capping. Cut it out to the shape of your Heel, but slightly over-size. Two short pieces of white/black/white Purfling are bent and glued into a rebate so that they will join up neatly with the Side Purfling (20.11). Glue the Capping with Cascamite or P.V.A., holding it down with a cramp (20.12).

31   Round off all the sharp corners of the Edgings and Heel Capping to the same radius.

The Sound-board is dealt with in the same way as the Back (20.13 and 20.14), but it is easier because there are fewer mitred joints to make in the Purfling inlays; they are simply butted together on the centre-line of the Sound-board. The inlay used around the edges is made up from black/white/black strips to contrast with the spruce, with an added white strip next to the rosewood Edgings (20.1). Make up these inlays first (refer to Chapter 17), then bend them on the iron. The white strip can be either a piece of sycamore veneer scraped down to ½mm (20.15), or it can be planed from the edge of a thicker piece of white wood. It is possible to make your own inlays from many different varieties of softwood in this way. The plane must be very sharp, and set (by experiment) to produce a shaving ½mm thick. It will be curled up when it comes out of the plane, but can be ironed flat. Hand-made hardwood inlays, however, can only be scraped down to the desired thickness. The simple but effective pull-through for thinning all types of inlay is described in Chapter 4. You can make one in a few minutes.

The width of the rebate to accommodate the Sound-board Purfling and Edging will be 4mm (2mm inlay plus 2mm Edging). At the top of the Sound-board, 10mm notches are cut to receive the ends of the strips; these will eventually be covered by the Finger-board (20.16).

Sometimes the edge of the rebate breaks away in places, particularly when you are working with rosewood. Don't be disheartened if this happens, because you can repair the damage quite easily. After gluing in the strips but before paring them down, make up a filler to match the wood that has been damaged, by rubbing an off-cut on a file. Mix the wood dust to a stiff paste with P.V.A. glue, and fill the cavities just above the level of the

20.13 **Cutting the rebate for the Sound-board Purfling**

20.14 **Fitting the Sound-board Edging and Side Purfling**

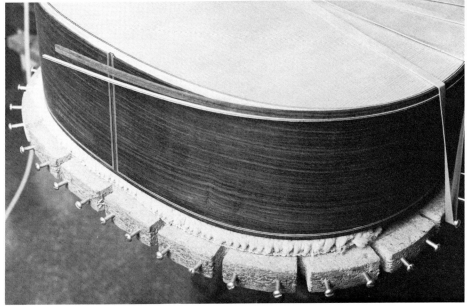

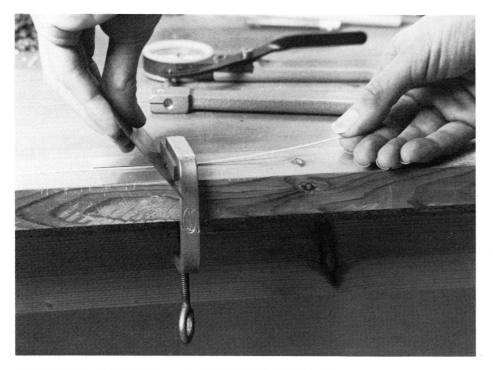

20.15 **An additional white strip being prepared for the Sound-board Purfling**

20.16 **Notching in the ends of the strips**

surrounding surface. When you have scraped the inlays (and any fillings) down smoothly, the damage will be hardly noticeable, especially on rosewood.

The sound-chamber of your guitar is now complete, and the next operation involves the fitting and gluing of the Finger-board.

21   THE FINGER-BOARD

The finest guitars usually have an ebony Finger-board, but you may prefer to use rosewood for your first guitar; Indian rosewood is easily obtainable, less expensive than ebony, and not quite as difficult to prepare. Ebony, however, is very handsome and hard-wearing, but it is also very brittle and must be treated with great care. They are both beautiful woods, and whichever you decide upon, the method of preparation is the same.

1   Plane the wood on both sides and then examine it carefully, choosing the best surface for the top.

2   Check that the Finger-board is not twisted. The slightest warp is made clearly visible by resting two straight battens on their edges, one at each end of the Finger-board, and sighting across them. A small discrepancy can be corrected by planing diagonally across the two high corners. A large degree of twist will be impossible to remove without over-thinning the Finger-board, and the timber will have to be replaced, so it is important to inspect your materials closely as soon as they arrive, as pointed out in Chapter 2.

3   Plane and scrape your chosen surface until it is perfectly smooth and flat in all directions.

4   Mark your top face for identification, and draw a centre line from top to bottom with a soft pencil so that you will not indent the surface.

5   Draw the outlines using the dimensions shown in *21.1* (54mm at the Nut, and 64mm at the half-scale position).

6   Plane the edges of the Finger-board to your outline.

7   Gauge the thickness of 7mm on the edges, and plane the waste off the back of the board, levelling it at the same time.

8   Square up the top end so that it forms an exact right-angle with the centre-line.

9 Before shaping the lower end to the curve of the Sound-hole, the Finger-board must be carefully fitted to the slight angle between Neck and Sound-board. To do this, first position your Finger-board on the Neck so that the top end lies exactly 33cm from the half-scale (Neck/Sides joint) position thus forming the 5mm slot for the ivory Nut. Draw a line across the Neck at this point.

10 Mark the position on the edges of the Finger-board, where the angle changes, i.e. at the joint between Neck and Sides.

11 On the under-surface, draw a line across the Finger-board at a right-angle to the centre-line, where the angle changes.

12 Begin the fitting by tapering the lower end of the under-surface with a smoothing plane, working slowly, and constantly testing the fit. The gap between the Finger-board and the Neck at the half-scale position will indicate the maximum amount of wood that has to be removed. Light sanding may be necessary on the Neck and Sound-board down to the edge of the Sound-hole to form a perfect gluing surface.

13 Shine a light behind the edge of the Neck with the Finger-board in place. No light should show through the joint. A badly fitted Finger-board will distort the Neck. Achieving a really close contact between these two large surfaces can be very troublesome. The most common fault is 'sideways rock', caused by a slight rounding of the faces during fitting. If you are aware of the problem from the start, you will probably be able to avoid this trouble. To cure it once it has developed, inspect the joint closely in order to discover the exact cause, and then, checking constantly, gradually remove the offending bumps.

14 Clamp your Finger-board in its exact position on the Neck. Two long straight battens must now be held at the sides of the Finger-board. The distances from the inner edges of the battens to the centre joint at the bottom of the Sound-board, are then measured with dividers (21.2). Readjust the Finger-board position if necessary, to even up these measurements exactly.

15 Mark the Sound-board and Neck very lightly at both sides of the Finger-board to indicate its gluing position, and draw round the edge of the Sound-hole to mark the lower extremity.

21.2 **Checking the alignment of the Finger-board**

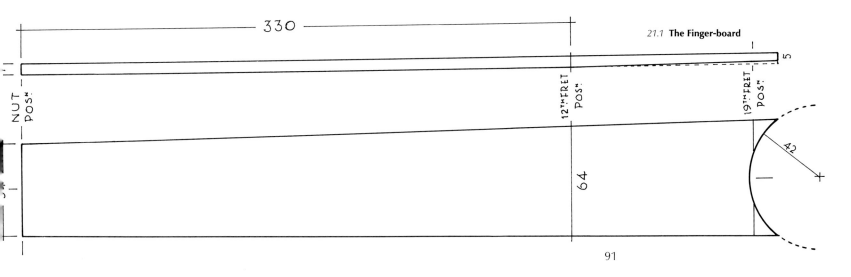

21.1 **The Finger-board**

330

NUT POSⁿ

12ᵀᴴ FRET POSⁿ

19ᵀᴴ FRET POSⁿ

5

64

42

16 Remove the Finger-board and cut out the lower end with a coping saw, smoothing the curve with a round file and sanding-stick.

Procedures differ widely from one maker to another; some saw the fret slots before gluing on the Finger-board, whilst others complete the fretting entirely in advance. There are advantages in both of these methods, but I feel that the risk of misplaced fretting by a slight movement of the Finger-board when gluing, rules them out. Added to this, a Finger-board that has had its frets hammered in before being glued to the Neck, could be badly warped, increasing the difficulties of fitting later on. My advice, therefore, is to glue the Finger-board on first.

17 A little preparatory work is well worth while. The gluing area is very large and consequently a lot of glue must be squeezed from this broad area through the sides of the joint. The Finger-board loves to slide about on this wet glue after it has been clamped, finally settling happily where you least want it! Some means of restricting its

21.3 **Dowelling the joint between Neck and Finger-board**

21.4 **Gluing on the Finger-board**

freedom must be found. The Nut slot can be blocked by a false Nut formed from a piece of wood to the exact thickness of the final ivory Nut (5mm). Sideways movement can be prevented by clamping the two battens to the body of your guitar with the Finger-board in position, removing it to apply the glue, then dropping it back in place.

Another time-honoured method of dealing with this kind of problem is 'secret' dowelling, and it is used by the Spanish luthier, José Romanillos. Two small dowels are glued into the upper face of the Neck, and these fit into matching holes in the underside of the Finger-board (21.3). The exact locations for the dowels are found by tapping two ordinary dressmaker's pins into the Neck (position them on the centre-line about 3cm from each end). Clip them off leaving about 1mm protruding, position your Finger-board accurately over the pins and press it down to mark the positions for the dowel holes. Drill the holes in the underside of the Finger-board with a 2mm twist drill but be extremely careful to go no deeper than 2mm. Extract the pins from the Neck with pliers and drill the 2mm holes for the dowels. (You can go a little deeper here, but remember that the Neck will be thinned down in the final shaping). Glue the dowels into the Neck, and cut and file them to within about 1½mm of the surface. Test the fit of the Finger-board to make certain that it will press right down on to the Neck.

The clamping arrangement must be planned in advance. 21.4 illustrates the usual method. The part of the Finger-board which covers the Sound-board must be provided with a clamping block positioned beneath the Sound-board, avoiding the struts. The entire length of the upper surface can be covered by a single, flat, clamping batten, but I prefer a combination of G cramps with pieces of cork for protection, and a binding of strong string or tape.

18 Try out the complete set-up in a dry state. When you are quite satisfied, coat the underside of your Finger-board and the Neck with Cascamite mixed to a slightly thinner consistency than usual. This will slow up the setting a little to give you more time to get the cramps on, and it will also produce a closer joint because more glue will be squeezed out. Press your Finger-board into place, clamping and binding it down tightly. You *must* remember to remove the false Nut and the positioning battens (if you use this method), *before the glue sets hard*! Scrape away the gelled glue from all the edges (not forgetting the Nut slot and the edge of the Sound-hole), and clean everything up thoroughly with a damp cloth. Leave the cramps on for at least six hours in a warm room.

22 FRETTING

Many guitars of the past (and some quite expensive models of the present) have incorrectly spaced fretting, and their owners can never play in tune no matter how carefully they adjust the strings. You will not be one of them!

The nineteen metal Frets on a classical guitar Finger-board are set at intervals of a semitone from the Nut to the Sound-hole. They are fitted into slots cut with a saw. Obviously, these saw-cuts must be positioned with great accuracy. Unfortunately, it's not just a question of setting a pair of dividers to a semitone spacing, and 'walking' them up the Finger-board; the distances between the Frets diminish as they go higher.

The important factor in the calculation of these measurements is the scale-length, and as this dimension can vary from one guitar to another, so fretting intervals will also differ. The guitar featured in this book has a scale-length of 66cm, and the following measurements are given *for this scale-length only*. If your scale-length differs, refer to the section at the end of this chapter.

Some makers shape and smooth the Neck before commencing the fretting. I prefer to leave the Neck in its rough state as long as possible so that I can continue putting cramps on it and gripping it firmly in a vice without having to worry about bruising a finished surface. However, it is a good idea to trim the sides of the Neck flush with the Finger-board at this stage to provide a clear run for the sliding bevel.

1 Clamp your guitar to the bench in such a way that the Neck is firmly held. A small portable vice is useful for this.

2 Check with a straight-edge to ensure that the Finger-board is perfectly flat, because this is your last chance to make any minor corrections. If it does need levelling, use your longest plane, sharpened like a razor, and set as fine as it will go. I find that the best way to do this is to retract the blade so that it does not cut at all,

and then to turn the adjustment wheel a fraction at a time until you are just beginning to take off the finest shaving.

The Finger-boards on some top-grade instruments are reduced in height on the bass (left-hand) side by about 1½mm. This slight taper is gradual; from nil at the Nut, to maximum at the Sound-hole, whilst the level across the Finger-board remains perfectly flat at all positions. The reason for this adjustment is to allow more freedom of movement for the bass strings, without the need to increase the height of the Bridge Saddle unduly. A low 'action' on the bass side causes the strings to buzz annoyingly against the Frets. As you can imagine, this is a very exacting and time-consuming task, and is probably better avoided for your first guitar unless you are already a skilled craftsman. It is common practice to cure 'buzzing' by varying the height of the Saddle from treble to bass, giving it a slight upwards slope. This is done by trial and error when adjusting the 'action' of the strings, to be described in Chapter 26.

3 Wipe the surface with a wet cloth and allow it to dry. This causes the grain to rise, and after sanding the surface smooth again, re-dampen the Finger-board. Continue doing this until the grain no longer rises. This procedure ensures that the surface will remain smooth in spite of perspiring fingers. The Finger-board is never varnished.

SCALE-LENGTH: 660mm

	mm
Nut to 1st Fret	37·0
Nut to 2nd Fret	72·0
Nut to 3rd Fret	105·0
Nut to 4th Fret	136·2
Nut to 5th Fret	165·6
Nut to 6th Fret	193·3
Nut to 7th Fret	219·5
Nut to 8th Fret	244·2
Nut to 9th Fret	267·6
Nut to 10th Fret	289·6
Nut to 11th Fret	310·4
Nut to 12th Fret	330·0 (half-scale position)
Nut to 13th Fret	348·5
Nut to 14th Fret	366·0
Nut to 15th Fret	382·5
Nut to 16th Fret	398·1
Nut to 17th Fret	412·8
Nut to 18th Fret	426·7
Nut to 19th Fret	439·8 (divided fret)

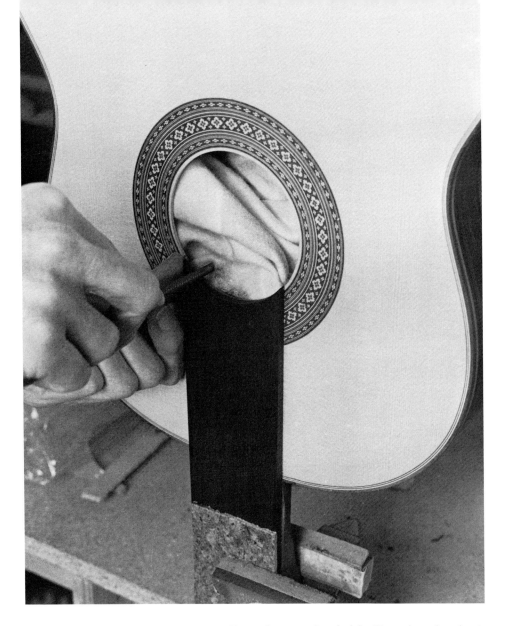

7   Set your sliding bevel to run along the edge of the Finger-board, making a perfect right-angle with the centre-line. To test the setting for accuracy, draw a pencil line across, turn the bevel over, and place it against the opposite edge; the line must coincide.

8   Put the point of the knife in the 1st Fret incision and slide the bevel up to touch it.

9   Hold the bevel down firmly or put a small cramp on it, and make a knife cut across the Finger-board.

10   Repeat 8 and 9 at every Fret position. The 19th Fret is in two sections on either side of the Sound-hole (See 21.1).

When dealing with the 12th to 19th Frets, it is a wise precaution to protect the Sound-board on each side by taping on two thin metal or plastic sheets.

Fret-wire has a 'T' section with a rounded top. The tang which fits into the slots in the Finger-board is usually embossed with small studs to grip the sides of the slots (22.2). The saw you use to cut the slots must have fine teeth, set to make a cut of the right width to grip the Frets. A small back-saw similar to the one illustrated in 22.3 should produce the correct width, or you may prefer to use a dove-tail saw. The only way is to experiment with a spare piece of ebony or rosewood until you can hammer in a trial piece of fret-wire that will hold securely.

11   Clamp your sliding bevel in position at the 1st Fret so that the saw will run alongside it, making a cut exactly on your knife-cut.

12   You can set the depth of the saw-cut by fixing a strip of wood to the side of the saw-blade with small cramps, but I find that this restricts one's view, so I keep testing the depth with the end of a thin rule. A narrow strip of zinc or aluminium with the required depth marked across its end would serve equally well. Just under 2mm is about right. Test the depth on your spare piece of wood, making sure that the slot is deep enough to allow the fret-wire to 'seat' accurately on the face of the Finger-board without gaps, but not so deep as to leave a gap under the wire; this would also weaken the Finger-board unnecessarily.

22.1 Perfecting the end of the Finger-board

22.2

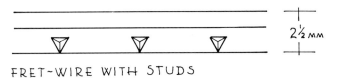

4   Shape the curved end of the Finger-board so that it is flush with the edge of the Sound-hole (22.1).

5   Re-draw the centre-line, and clamp to the Finger-board a good quality steel rule or measuring tape with millimetre markings, placing the zero mark exactly at the top end (the Nut position).

6   With the point of a Stanley knife, make a small incision at each Fret measurement, estimating the tenths of a millimetre as closely as you can. It is advisable to double-check all these measurements.

13   Cut each slot slowly and carefully with the saw pressed against the sliding bevel (22.3).

14   With wire-cutters, cut nineteen Frets from your coil of fret-wire allowing about a centimetre of waste on each Fret. Be sure to straighten the coil before you begin cutting. This is a rather tedious job which must be done by hand; the use of pliers or a vice could damage the soft metal.

15   Starting at the 1st Fret, with the Neck resting on a block of wood below the slot, press in the Fret as far as the studs. (Frets are normally fitted dry, but some makers use a little glue as insurance against the annoyance of a loose Fret later on.)

16   Hammer the Fret in with light taps, being careful not to tilt the hammer head and bruise the Finger-board (22.4). If your hammer marks the fret-wire, dome the head slightly with a file, and polish it with emery paper. Another way is to protect the Fret with a piece of hardwood, but unfortunately this absorbs a lot of the force of the blows. Make certain that the ends of the Fret are tapped well home.

17   Continue up the Finger-board until you reach the Frets over the Sound-board, re-positioning the block of

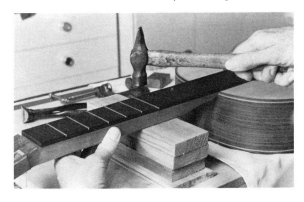

wood each time, so that it is below the Fret you are working on. The 13th and 14th Frets are well supported by the Top Block, but you will have to provide support inside the guitar before hammering in the final five Frets. A large block of hardwood can be held underneath the Sound-board through the Sound-hole. A better way is to fit a clamping block around the struts underneath the Sound-board, and to squeeze in the Frets with a cramp (22.5). This avoids hammering over the Sound-board which could loosen a strut.

18   Clip off the waste with wire-cutters (22.6), and file the ends down flush with the edges of the Finger-board (22.7). You will find this very enjoyable.

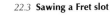
22.3   **Sawing a Fret slot**

22.5   **Using a cramp on the last few Frets**

22.6   **Clipping off the ends**

22.7   **Filing the ends flush with the Finger-board**

22.4   **Hammering in the Frets**

Fretting calculations for a different scale-length

If your scale-length is working out differently, or if at some time you wish to make a guitar with a scale-length of, say, 65cm, you must re-calculate your Fret spacings. This can be done in the following way:

1   Measure your half-scale length in millimetres from the top end of the Finger-board to the point where the Neck joins the Sides (the 12th Fret).

2   Double this measurement to find the full scale-length. (String-length is usually slightly longer than this, because of the compensation addition described later in Chapter 24.)

3   Divide the full scale-length measurement by the divisor 17·817 to give you the distance from the top of

22.8 Levelling the Frets

22.9 Rounding the tops of the Frets

19   The Frets must now be 'dressed' by first rubbing an oil-stone across them to ensure that they are level (22.8), and then by shaping each Fret with a needle file or a special fret-file and fine emery paper until their tops are uniformly rounded. Masking tape is used to protect the surface of the Finger-board during this operation (22.9), and it is also a wise precaution to protect the face of the Sound-board. The divided Fret at the 19th position must have its inner ends filed to conform to the curve of the Sound-hole.

20   Finally, all the corners of the Frets must be slightly rounded, so that your hand can slide painlessly up and down the Finger-board.

Finger-boards are not varnished, but they can be rubbed with linseed oil. The oil dries out, but it enhances the colour of the wood. Ebony sometimes has light streaks running through it; these can be toned down with a proprietary ebonising stain before any oiling is done.

the Finger-board to the centre of the 1st Fret. You will need a pocket calculator as you must be accurate to three places of decimals.

4   Subtract this 1st Fret distance from the scale-length, and divide the remainder by 17·817 again to give you the distance from the 1st Fret to the 2nd Fret.

5   Add the 1st and 2nd Fret measurements together to give the distance from the top of the Finger-board to the centre of the 2nd Fret.

6   Subtract this distance (1st plus 2nd Fret) from the scale-length and divide by 17·817 to provide the 3rd fret measurement.

7   Continue up the Finger-board in this way to the 19th fret. Check at the 12th Fret that the measurement tallies with your half-scale length, if not, I'm afraid you have made an error in your calculations, and you will have to start again.

clearly for identification. Work slowly, testing the section with your templates frequently as you approach the final shape (23.3).

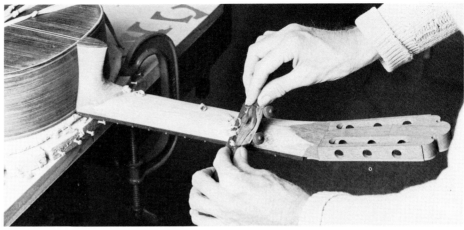

23.1 **Shaping the Neck with a spokeshave**

23 SHAPING THE NECK

You have now reached the final stages in the construction of your guitar. All that remains is to shape the Neck and finish to perfection all the surfaces and edges before gluing on the Bridge and varnishing.

1 Fix the body of your guitar firmly to the work-board with several rubber bands. The Head and Neck must project over the edge of the board.

2 With a spokeshave, begin to shape the back of the Neck (23.1). It gradually tapers towards the Head, and the most accurate way to achieve a uniform section is to make four templates, one for each end and two for the middle of the Neck. The best material to use for templates is thin zinc. It is soft enough to be cut very easily with a fret-saw and then shaped accurately with a file. Make four—one each for the Nut position and the 3rd, 6th and 9th Fret positions (23.2). Mark them very

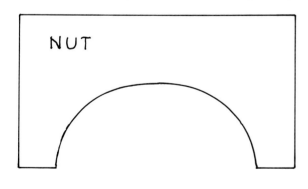

23.3 **Testing the shape at the 6th Fret**

NUT

3

FULL SIZE

6

9

23.2 **Neck templates**

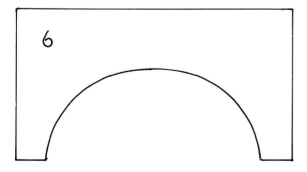

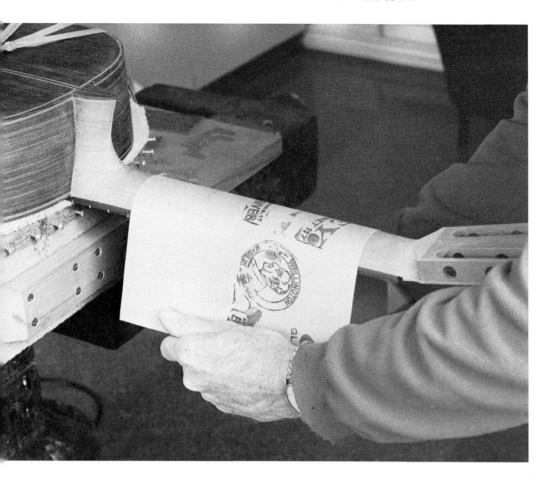

7   Carefully work over the whole instrument, slightly rounding all the edges. The body Edgings must be finished to an evenly rounded shape, and smoothed with the finest sandpaper; also the outside edge of the Sound-hole, and the edges of the Head.

8   Finally, rub down and polish the complete guitar with flour-paper, removing all file marks and sandpaper scratches, until you are quite satisfied that your creation is ready for varnishing. To avoid soiling the Sound-board surface, rub down the darker woods first. Use a fresh piece of flour-paper for the spruce, dampening the surface to raise the grain, allowing time for it to dry thoroughly, and then rubbing down. Do this repeatedly until the grain ceases to rise.

The tuning machines should be fitted and screwed on at this stage, but they must be removed, of course, before you begin varnishing. Position them carefully, so that the side-plates are perfectly in line with the sides of the Head, and ensure that the rollers are free to rotate easily in their sockets. Mark the Head through the fixing holes and bore very small, shallow pilot holes for the tiny screws. Screw on your machines using round-headed screws to match the colour of the side-plates. If you are a perfectionist, polish the screw-heads and give them a dab of varnish.

23.4 **Perfecting the rounded shape**

3   The edges of the Finger-board are included in the rounded section of the Neck, and when you are close to the finished shape, change to a fine sanding stick. A straight-edge must be laid along the Neck, and any bumps and hollows carefully evened out.

4   A very simple, and labour-saving method of achieving a perfectly rounded shape to the underside of the Neck, is to use a whole sheet of medium-grade sandpaper as shown in *23.4*.

5   The trickiest parts are at the Heel and Head. The transition from the Neck section into the Heel must be perfectly rounded and smooth (*23.3*). You will find that your round-section sanding sticks and round files are invaluable for this final shaping. At the Head, the underside can be shaped to a symmetrical double curve as shown in *23.4*, the Neck rounding smoothly into it.

6   Shape and smooth the Heel to perfection, paying particular attention to the joint with the body. This is another situation where a template can be used to advantage; the opposite sides of the Heel must be perfectly symmetrical where they meet the Sides (*23.3*).

24 THE BRIDGE

At first sight, the Bridge appears to be a complicated and difficult thing to make, but you will discover that it is quite simple when you begin to follow the sequence of operations. Once again, it is a matter of care and patience as in all the other aspects of guitar construction. Three stages in Bridge making are shown in 24.1.

1 Plane and square up your rosewood or ebony Bridge blank to the dimensions given in 24.2.

2 Mark out the centre-section from the measurements on to your chosen top surface, and score the lines with a Stanley knife.

3 Gauge the maximum thickness of the wings (4mm) on the sides and ends, but not across the centre-section.

4 With a paring chisel, make small grooves alongside the knife cuts at the ends of the centre-section in the waste area over the wings. These provide a guide for the back-saw, and also result in clean ends to the centre-section.

5 Grip the blank in a vice, covering the jaws with pieces of soft cardboard if necessary, and make saw-cuts at the ends of the centre-section down to the gauged line.

6 Saw away the waste portions over the wings.

7 Gauge the width of the string Tie-block on the centre-section, score and groove as before, and make a saw-cut almost down to the surface of the wings. Don't forget to gauge the position of the rear 'lip' at the base of the Tie-block.

8 Gauge the position of the 2mm wide Bridge Saddle slot.

9 Form the string threading ramp by either sawing at the correct angle down to the base of the Tie-block, or by chiselling the waste away (24.3).

10 Cut the Bridge Saddle slot by the 'scoring, grooving and sawing' technique, clearing the slot with your fine purfling groove chisel.

11 The under surface of the Bridge must now be hollowed out to fit the arched face of the Sound-board. Place it in its approximate position by measuring 66cm from the top of the Finger-board to the Saddle slot, then measure the gaps under the ends of the Bridge; this indicates the maximum amount of wood which must be removed from the centre to provide a concave gluing surface. The fitting must be very exact because of the important relationship between the Bridge and the Sound-board.

24.1 **Three stages in Bridge making**

24.3 **Cutting the ramp**

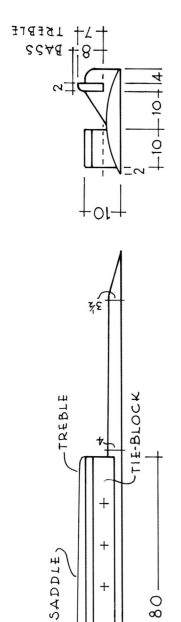

FULL SIZE

24.2 **The Bridge and the Nut**

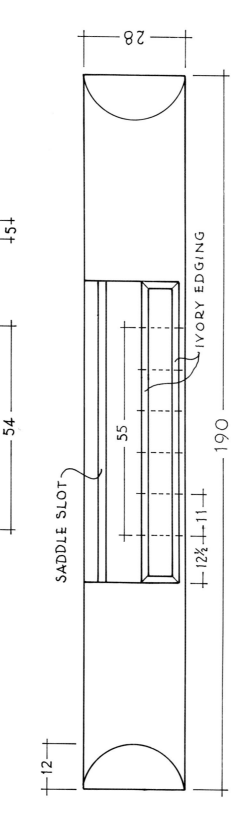

12   The edges of the Tie-block must now be inlayed with thin strips of ivory to protect them from damage caused by the tension of the strings. Sometimes, strips of decorative Purfling are let into the edges of the Block. Another method is to cap the top of the Tie-block with a single piece of ivory about 1mm thick; this can be seen on some of Torres' guitars. The Tie-block in the illustration is being framed with ivory strips, having previously been covered with a veneer of rosewood to match the Head facing. The corners of the frame are neatly mitred. Some makers decorate the top of the Tie-block with a piece of their Rosette mosaic. The ivory edgings are glued with Araldite into grooves scored with a knife and then chiselled out (*24.4*).

13   Shape the curved tops of the wings with a chisel and file (*24.5*). The edges of the wings are not quite thinned to a feather edge, but very nearly so. At the same time, shape the 'lip' behind the Tie-block to 'follow through' between the wings.

24.4 **A large paper clip serves as a cramp for the Tie-block edgings**

24.5 **Shaping the wings**

100

14 Cut the wings to length and form the ramps at the ends with a flat file so that they present a semi-circular shape in plan view.

15 Cut the Bridge Saddle and Nut from a piece of ivory (24.6). Ivory cuts fairly easily with a hacksaw, and can be shaped with a file and then polished with fine emery paper. Gradually rub down the sides of the Nut and Saddle on a file until they just press into their slots; they must never be glued because they need to be removed occasionally to readjust the height of the strings above the Frets. Round off the appropriate edges and corners as in the diagrams, and make the string grooves in the Nut with a round-sectioned needle file to the precise spacing given in the diagram. They should be half string thickness in depth. Note that the grooves are of different widths to accommodate the varying string thicknesses from bass to treble. The Bridge Saddle is never grooved.

16 The string Tie-block must now be drilled with six holes. If you possess a vertical bench drill it can be put to good use here, otherwise you will either have to use a wheel brace, or concoct a make-shift drilling jig similar to the one illustrated in 24.7. The electric drill, held in its drill-stand, runs along the edge of a steel rule clamped to the bench. The Bridge, clamped to its supporting block, is gripped in a small portable vice which also runs along the edge of the bench, but at a right-angle to the rule. Use a spirit-level to set up the jig accurately. Mark the positions of the holes very clearly because the all-important spacing of the six strings is dependent upon this 11mm measurement. Glue a strip of white paper to the back of the Tie-block so that your marking will be easier to see. Prick the holes with a compass point and start them by hand with a 1½mm twist drill. Note that the string holes pierce the Tie-block in such a position that they emerge at the base of the ramp.

17 Smooth and polish your Bridge with the finest sandpaper, preparing it for gluing to the Sound-board.

18 Mark the back of the Tie-block at the exact centre point between the 3rd and 4th string holes.

19 Clean the Sound-board in the area of the Bridge with fine sandpaper, and place the Bridge, complete with its Saddle, in position on the centre joint of the Sound-board. Now you must apply 'compensation'. The added tension when a string is pressed down to the Finger-board causes a slight sharpening of the note, but this problem is easily overcome by increasing the vibrating length of the strings. The inner (nearest to the Sound-hole) edge of the Saddle should first be positioned exactly 66cm from the inner (nearest to the Sound-hole) edge of the Nut, then you must move the Bridge back towards the bottom end of your guitar a distance of 2mm giving a total string-length of 66.2cm.

20 Check that the Bridge is at an exact right-angle to the centre joint, hold it firmly and indicate its position with a small pencil mark at each corner.

24.7 **A simple but effective drilling jig**

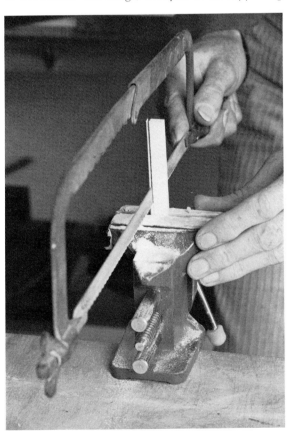

24.6 **Cutting ivory for the Saddle and Nut**

21 Using your three, deep-throated guitar-makers' cramps, and the Bridge clamping block (prepared in Chapter 16), test the clamping of the Bridge to familiarise yourself with the procedure before applying the glue (24.8). The clamping block can be wedged lightly in place inside the guitar with two small pieces of hardboard between the Back and the block.

24.8 **Gluing on the Bridge**

22 With the Bridge clamped in position, drill two small holes through the bottom of the Saddle slot into the Sound-board, placing them as far apart as possible but avoiding drilling into the fan struts. After unclamping, glue a small piece of dowel into each hole in the Bridge; this will prevent it from sliding on the wet glue.

23 Clean the gluing surface of the Bridge thoroughly, and spread a thin coating of Cascamite on the Sound-board and the back of the Bridge, locate the dowels and press it firmly into place. Apply the cramps, wiping away squeezed-out glue. Leave the cramps on for at least six hours.

Some makers put the strings on at this stage and make small changes to the thickness of the Sound-board in certain areas to improve the response. It is only after many years of experience, however, that you can know exactly where to make these adjustments to produce the sound you want; they will also vary from one guitar to another. I would not advise the beginner to follow this procedure on his first guitar.

25 VARNISHING AND POLISHING

Many thousands of words have been written about the varnishing of stringed instruments, and all makers from Stradivari up to the present day have had their pet theories. Great mystery and secrecy surrounded many of the procedures and formulas of the past, and as a result, some wonderful ideas have no doubt been lost for ever. The advantages and disadvantages of certain types of varnish are still hotly debated, but one aspect seems to reveal itself clearly where guitars are concerned; this has to do with the quantity, rather than the type, of varnish applied. Putting on layer after layer deadens the response, so my advice is to put on as few coats as possible to achieve an even, protective surface.

The traditional finishes come under the headings of oil or spirit based varnishes, and French polish. (I have included a section on French polishing at the end of this chapter.) Many of today's top luthiers are now using lacquer on their instruments. The advantages of these modern materials are not yet fully appreciated by makers of hand-made instruments, but guitar factories have been using them for years. For commercial reasons, factories use a spraying and machine-polishing technique, and an over generous thickness of lacquer is usually the result. The individual craftsman, however, can use all his skill and time to produce a perfect finish by brushing on the thinnest coating possible, and then hand-polishing. The final surface can be left matt or semi-matt, or it can be brought to a high gloss; from a protection point of view there is little to choose between them but a gloss finish is easier to keep clean. The end result is a scratch-resistant, moisture-proof surface which is unaffected by oils or spirits.

The lacquer comes in two parts—resin and hardener—which are mixed together in the proportions given by the manufacturer just before you are ready to start varnishing. The mixture does not keep; any left over must be discarded. Try to judge the quantity you will need for each coat, but don't risk running out of lacquer in the middle of a coat, because each one must be applied quickly in one operation.

Special thinners are used, and you must wash your brush in these very thoroughly after the final application. The brush can be left suspended in the thinners between coats, however, because with this type of finish, one coat can follow another quite quickly. In fact, you are usually required to re-coat within twenty-four hours. With traditional varnish you must wait a week or more between the successive applications. Oil varnish can take months to harden completely, especially on rosewood, where the oils in the wood seem to have a retarding effect on the drying process.

The finishing of a musical instrument can be divided into three distinct operations: staining, grain filling, and varnishing, so before any varnish is applied to your guitar, you must decide whether you wish to stain the Sound-board, or leave it with a natural finish. It is entirely a matter of personal preference, but, unless you are going to use an oil or spirit varnish which can be tinted, any colouring must be done first. Best quality artists' water colour is the easiest to apply, and an infinite variety of tints can be mixed and tried out on an off-cut of spruce. First, try a golden yellow called 'gamboge'. The water colour will raise the grain, however, unless you take the necessary precautions, so make certain that you give your Sound-board the treatment described in Chapter 23, Instruction 8. The aim is to achieve an even tint over the whole surface; some makers use a wad of cotton-wool, others a brush. Choose the method which suits you best. A thin wash of colour is all that is required, but make sure that you mix a sufficient quantity to cover the whole area in one operation, allowing for soakage into the porous surface. If you ran out of the mixture it would be impossible to match the colour exactly, but even if you could, the join would show and the final effect would be streaky. Spread the colour on with long, smooth strokes, following the grain of the spruce.

Next comes filling. Inspect the surfaces of your Back and Sides closely. If you have used maple the grain should not require filling, but rosewood has an open-pored structure, and these cavities must be filled before any lacquer is applied. Special fillers must be obtained from the suppliers of the lacquer, and these are available in a variety of wood colours. Protect any light coloured Purflings or Edgings with narrow strips of masking tape, and cover the Sound-board (which is never filled) with a sheet of clean paper, taped around the edges. Rub the filler well into the open pores with a piece of sacking (obtainable from a green-grocer), working across the direction of the grain. Sometimes the Head and Neck also need to be filled. A lighter colour will be required for these parts. After a few

minutes (not longer, or the filler will have become too hard), rub off the surface filler with the sacking, again working across the grain, leaving as much filler as possible in the pores of the wood. Always allow the specified time for the material to set hard before rubbing down, or your abrasive paper will immediately clog up and become useless. If, after rubbing down, the surface is still not quite free from holes, a further treatment with filler will be necessary. It is well worth the time and effort involved to achieve a faultless surface at this early stage.

1   Buy a soft haired varnishing brush about 2½cm in width. The bristles of an ordinary house-painting brush are too stiff.

2   Suspend your guitar from a hook in the ceiling in a position where it is free from obstruction. It is essential to keep the room as dust-free as possible.

3   Mix the priming coat with thinners to the maker's instructions, dip a small piece of rag in the mixture, and wipe over every part of your guitar. This is known as a 'tack-rag', and it removes every particle of dust adhering to the surface.

4   Brush on your priming coat with long, even strokes, first to the Sound-board, then the Back, followed by the Sides, working from the Heel down to the Bottom Joint. Finish with the Head, Neck and Heel in that order. The Finger-board is always left unvarnished.

5   After 24 hours the priming coat is ready to receive the first full coat. Smooth the surface all over very lightly with fine grade 'wet or dry' carborundum paper, *used dry*. (The primed surface is not completely waterproof.) This light rubbing will remove little 'nibs' that would increase in size with the following coat.

6   Wipe over the whole guitar thoroughly with a tack-rag.

7   Mix the varnish for your first full coat without thinners, using the exact proportions given, and apply it in the same order as before. Hold the instrument with one hand through the Sound-hole, placing your thumb on the Finger-board. Keep what is known as a 'wet edge' whilst varnishing, by working systematically across the large areas of the Sound-board and Back, and apply the varnish fairly liberally. 'Brush-out' the minimum necessary to achieve a run-free surface. Avoid going back over a partially dried area; runs which have been allowed to develop unnoticed are better left alone. Rub these down when the coat is quite dry. When varnishing the Head, treat the insides of the string slots and the edges first, then the back and front

facing. Watch out for runs, and do not varnish the slot for the Nut.

8 Wait for another 24 hours before rubbing down wet. This is done using fine 'wet or dry' paper dipped in water, and it causes a white 'slurry' to collect on the surface. This must be constantly wiped away with a damp sponge. Treat a small area at a time, wiping away the slurry and drying with a dry cloth so that you can see the result. You won't achieve an all-over matt surface on this thin coating of varnish without the risk of going through to the wood, so be content with a general 'flattening-down'. Be careful on edges and corners (these rub through very easily) but don't worry if you go through here and there at this stage.

9 Before applying the second full coat, rub over the complete guitar using the paper dry. This creates a 'keyed' surface for the next coat. Repeat instructions 7 and 8, and finish with another dry rub down.

10 Apply the third coat, and when the 24 hours have elapsed, you are ready to start work on the final surfacing. You have now built up a sufficient 'body' of varnish to enable you to rub down (wet) to a perfect matt surface over the whole guitar. Rub the edges with great delicacy because if you go through the finish now, another coat of varnish will have to be applied. Don't forget the insides of the string slots and the exit ramps.

11 When you have produced a beautiful silky surface (with this coat or a fourth one), polish it with a rubbing compound of the type used on car bodies. A piece of felt works well, rubbed with a circular motion, treating a small area at a time. The more you rub, the glossier the finish. It is possible to achieve a glass-like surface by continued hard rubbing with liquid car polish (avoid the silicone variety).

12 Screw on the tuning machines and line up all the screw-slots.

Now at last after all those hours of painstaking work, your guitar is finished, the grain and colour of its wood glowing beneath the protective coats of varnish. All that remains is the fitting of the strings.

French polishing

For those who wish to follow the tradition of the masters, and French polish their guitars, here are a few generalisations about this highly specialised subject. It takes a lifetime's experience to produce a first-class French polisher, so don't expect perfection at the first attempt! I would strongly advise anyone wishing to use this method to practise on some off-cuts of rosewood

and spruce before setting to work on their guitar, although they may well find that an acceptable result can be achieved almost immediately.

French polish can be bought ready-made, but it is very easy to make up yourself. It is simply shellac dissolved in methylated spirits. Flaked shellac in small quantities can be obtained from a chemist. The most common is brown shellac, but try to obtain the golden coloured variety, known as orange shellac. To make up about a half-litre of polish, you will need a half-litre of methylated spirits and 150 grammes of shellac flakes. You need not be too exact with these proportions; add more shellac or more spirit to make the polish thicker or thinner.

Make up the polish in a glass jar or bottle with an air-tight stopper. Never use a metal container—the mixture would very likely turn black! Leave it for a day or two before using, giving it an occasional shake. A sediment forms at the bottom after having stood for some time; this is insoluble wax, and must be shaken in, not strained off, because it is an essential ingredient of the polish.

I have given the correct proportions of shellac flakes to methylated spirits to make up what is known in the trade as '3-pound cut shellac'. This really means a consistency of 3 pounds of shellac to one gallon of methylated spirits. Before use, the polish should be thinned down to '1-pound cut shellac', so pour some of the mixture into another bottle and stir in three times the volume of spirit. This thinner consistency is much more easily applied, it dries faster and builds up to a finer finish.

Any staining of the Sound-board must be completed, and absolutely dry, before starting to polish. The whole guitar can then be given a coat of 3-pound cut shellac with a brush to seal the surface before filling the grain of the Sides and Back. Luthiers generally make up their own filler for French polished work from a mixture of pumice powder, spirit stain (to match the colour of the wood), and a little shellac and raw linseed oil for binding purposes. Ready-made fillers are easily obtainable, however, and are rubbed into the grain in exactly the same way as previously described.

French polish is traditionally applied with a 'rubber'. This is made from a piece of unbleached wadding wrapped in a 25cm square of fine linen. The size of the rubber can vary, however, depending on the work being done. The wadding is soaked with polish, the linen cover is put on, and the rubber is passed systematically over the wood with quick circular, or figure-of-eight movements, making certain that the edges are well coated. The polish oozes through the cloth cover, being fed on to the surface and filtered of any impurities at the same time. Never pour polish directly on to the outside of the rubber. A few drops of clear mineral oil or raw linseed oil are used as a lubricant.

As with all these crafts, there is a 'knack'. The knack with French polishing involves using the right amount of pressure combined with smooth movement, and never allowing the rubber to remain stationary on the surface for even a fraction of a second, or it will certainly stick and ruin the finish. When there is a feeling of tackiness, immediately slide the rubber from the surface—never stop in mid-stroke. Apply a drop of oil to the rubber and continue. Re-charge the wadding periodically, and lubricate the rubber as soon as it begins to stick.

The surface dries in a few minutes, so a continuous build-up of polish can be maintained. When you reach a stage where the surface has acquired a good gloss, leave the polish to harden for a day, and then continue in the same way. You may find that a light rubbing down with flour-paper between polishing sessions improves the finish, but this is not always necessary when French polishing.

The rubber will become hard and unusable if it is left for any length of time, and ideally, a new one should be made before each session. If you put it into an air-tight jar, you can prolong its life considerably.

The final process must be delayed until the polish has been allowed to harden, and is called 'spiriting off'. Its object is to remove all the oil left behind by the rubber, and to give the work that famous, mirror-like gloss. A fresh rubber must be made up using two covering cloths, and the wadding charged with methylated spirits only. The covers are put on and all the surplus spirit is thoroughly squeezed out so that the surface of the rubber just feels slightly damp. It is much better to err on the side of too little spirit than too much, otherwise the polish will be softened. The technique is to rub with circular movements as before, lightly at first but gradually increasing the pressure as the spirit evaporates, ending with long, smooth strokes in the direction of the grain of the wood.

Another finishing method which you may prefer, involves the gradual thinning of the polish on the original rubber by the addition of small quantities of spirit as you proceed. Continue to rub as the spirit dries out. The oil is gradually removed from the surface and a high gloss begins to appear. The rubber sticks very easily at this stage, but you must not add more oil. It is easy to understand why this operation is called 'stiffing'! The art lies in keeping the rubber in constant motion, commencing the circular movements clear of the surface and lowering the moving rubber on to it. Lift the rubber from the surface in the same way. Finish with long, smooth, elliptical or figure-of-eight strokes.

The Back and Sides should be completely finished and allowed to harden for three or four days. The instrument can then rest safely on some soft material while the Sound-board is being attended to.

When French polishing the Sound-board, the Bridge is always in the way; this is why some luthiers polish first and glue the Bridge on afterwards (see Chapter 28). They mask off the exact area that the Bridge will occupy (with glued paper or tape), until the Sound-board polishing is practically finished. When using this method, I also protect the gluing surface of the Bridge with masking tape and brush on two thin sealing coats of shellac. After an hour or so it can be French polished with a very small rubber almost to completion. All the masking tape is then removed and the Bridge can be glued to the protected space on the Sound-board in the normal way.

If you have trouble with French polishing (and most makers do, at one time or another), it may be comforting to know that you can clean the whole thing off with spirit and start again without damaging the instrument. But if you have had no previous experience, and would still like to try this 'heart-breaking business' (as José Romanillos so aptly puts it), practise thoroughly. Go through the complete operation—staining, grain-filling, building up the polish and finishing. You will then stand every chance of producing a first-class job.

The Neck, Head and Heel are much more easily lacquered with a brush than polished with a rubber, and the treatment described in the first part of this chapter is strongly recommended, not only for its ease of application, but also for its ability to stand up to the constant friction of the left hand. Lacquer is also moisture-proof, whereas French polish tends to deteriorate in time from the effects of perspiration. Deal with the Neck, Head and Heel first, polishing them to a high gloss before French polishing the body.

26   STRINGING AND ADJUSTING

The classical guitar is always strung with nylon—*never* wire. The introduction of nylon strings after the Second World War, caused a revolution in the guitar playing world. Previously, gut was the only material available, and strings were forever fraying and breaking—often in the middle of a concert! Nylon strings are more reliable, do not fray, stay in tune better and last longer. It is also possible to obtain strings with differing degrees of tension, and it is worth experimenting with your particular instrument to discover which tension suits it best from a tonal point of view. If you are not a player yourself, a guitarist friend will be able to advise you.

Your set of strings will be in separate envelopes numbered 1 to 6. Strings 1, 2 and 3 are made of mono-filament nylon, and 4, 5 and 6 are of nylon floss wound with fine wire. Always fit good quality strings. Cheap strings give poor tone, and are often impossible to tune accurately for all positions on the Finger-board. This is because their thickness, and consequently their tension, varies along the length of the string.

String No. 1 is the thinnest and it is fitted on the right-hand, or treble side, of the Finger-board. Tie the string to the Tie-block of the Bridge by the method shown in 26.1, and to the 1st string roller as in 26.2. Leave the string fairly loose. Now fit the 6th, or bass string on the left-hand side, followed by the 2nd and 5th, then 3rd and 4th. Each string has its own roller, and as this arrangement is always followed, the player knows automatically which button to turn to adjust the tuning (26.2).

The Action

Tension the six strings so that they are fairly taut, but low in pitch. Check the height of the strings above the first fret; it should measure 1mm between the top of the fret and the under-surface of the strings. Measure the distance between the top of the 12th fret and the under-surface of the 1st string—it should measure

26.3 **The finished guitar**

3mm. Do the same with the 6th string—it should measure 4mm. Adjusting the action of the strings (i.e. their freedom of movement above the frets) entails removing the Bridge Saddle and Nut, and filing their bottom edges until the string height is correct at the 1st and 12th frets. This must be done gradually, with frequent testing. In some cases the Bridge itself may need to be reduced in height by one or two millimetres to allow the ivory Saddle to project sufficiently. This will depend upon factors built into the instrument such as the lift of the Neck, the thickness of the Finger-board, and the amount of doming given to the Sound-board. If this reduction is necessary, remove small shavings of wood from the top of the Saddle slot with a block plane, checking constantly with the Saddle until about 1½mm to 2mm of ivory is projecting at its lowest (treble) side. Reshape the ramp and re-polish, after masking off the Sound-board.

The action should be checked fairly often on a new instrument, because string tension on the Bridge gradually increases the dome of the Sound-board, consequently raising the strings higher over the Finger-board. String height should be kept constant at the 12th fret, because a 'high action' makes a guitar more difficult to play in tune, and a 'low action' causes buzzing on the lower frets, especially on the bass strings. The 5th and 6th strings oscillate more widely than the higher strings, so they need greater freedom of movement. This is the reason for the higher action on the bass side.

Don't be tempted to tune your new guitar up to concert pitch straight away. It must be allowed to become accustomed gradually to the strains and stresses placed upon it. Tune it provisionally to: 1st 'C' (middle 'C' on the piano); 2nd 'G'; 3rd 'E flat'; 4th 'B flat'; 5th 'F'; and 6th 'C'. Play it like this for a few days, adjusting the tuning frequently to maintain this pitch. It is two whole tones lower than concert pitch, and reduces the tension by several kilos. Over a period of two weeks, raise the pitch by a semitone at a time to the correct tuning of: 1st 'E'; 2nd 'B'; 3rd 'G'; 4th 'D'; 5th 'A'; 6th 'E'. When tuning, keep plucking the string as you turn the button. This will avoid the danger of over-tensioning.

If you are plagued by buzzing on the frets, check in the following way to discover whether it is caused by insufficient height of the Nut, or of the Saddle. Pluck the 'open' (unstopped) strings quite hard to produce a loud note. If buzzing occurs, it will almost certainly be on the 1st fret, indicating that the Nut is too low. Buzzing which occurs when the strings are stopped is caused by insufficient height of the Saddle. In either case, a new Nut or Saddle will have to be made because packing must never be inserted beneath these vital components.

Nothing can touch the excitement of plucking the strings for the first time. All your hard work has been leading up to the special moment when you hear the voice of your guitar. Its tone will improve with time and use, until it reaches maturity.

Renew the strings fairly frequently, depending upon the amount of wear they get.

I wish you joy with your new instrument.

PART 3

THE MASTER GUITAR MAKERS

27   ANTONIO TORRES (1817–1892)

TORRES (Antonio de Torres Jurado), was born at La Cañada de San Urbano, near Almería in Southern Spain. There are no clear records of his early life and training, but he started work as a carpenter further along the coast at Vera. Some say that he was taught guitar making by the great Spanish luthier, José Pernas, in Granada, but this is now in doubt. It seems certain, however, that he was well established as a luthier in his own right during the 1850s in Seville. It was here that he gained his reputation; the renowned concert guitarists, Julian Arcas and Francisco Tarrega played his guitars at their recitals.

After about 20 years work, financial difficulties forced him to look for some other means to support himself and his family, so he moved back to Almería where he ran a china shop. It wasn't long, though, before he resumed his guitar making, and by the early 1880s he had re-established himself at 80 calle Real, La Cañada, Almería.

Torres was a great experimenter. He also had the ability to see clearly what was best in the work of gifted makers in the past, such as Juan and José Pagés and Louis Panormo. He co-ordinated their ideas and then developed them a stage further in his own instruments. His guitars were larger, with wider upper and lower bouts, and a deeper body. These changes in shape influenced the performer's technique, enabling him to sit more comfortably with his guitar resting securely on his left thigh. He fitted a wider finger-board with a minimum of 5cm at the nut position; the resulting wider string spacing overcoming the difficulties of playing music with several parts. He re-designed the bridge, incorporating a string tie-block; this has been in use on all classical guitars to the present day. He also standardised the length of the strings at 65cm from nut to bridge saddle.

The greatest contribution Torres made to the guitar was his world famous sound-board strutting system. After numerous trials he finally adopted the seven fan-strut design that is still in use today. Radiating struts under the sound-board had been used long before Torres' time, and are believed to have been invented in the 1780s. A guitar by Juan Pagés, dated 1797, is the first known instrument to possess seven fan-struts. An early Torres (dated 1854) from his Seville period has seven, so he was obviously quick to exploit the possibilities of the idea. His refinement of the system helped enormously to improve the tone of the guitar, and in 1862 he demonstrated this by building an instrument with papier-mâché back and sides, but using a high quality spruce sound-board with the Torres strutting system (27.1). This guitar is in the Barcelona Conservatory. Unfortunately, it is in an unplayable condition, with a badly cracked sound-board, but it is reputed to have had an unusual and beautiful tone, although rather lacking in volume.

In common with all the best guitar makers, he was meticulous in the choice of his materials. Only the finest quality spruce would do for his sound-boards. He used several different species of wood for the backs and sides, however, including rosewood, maple and Spanish cypress. Some of his backs are made up from four pieces of wood jointed symmetrically.

Torres changed the whole style of guitar making both in Spain and throughout the rest of the world. His instruments had a refined appearance, a lack of ornate decoration and a superiority of tone which eventually became the standard on which all future designs were based, right up to the present day. Some of the finest instruments by modern luthiers are replicas of Torres guitars. The new sounds inspired composers, and encouraged gifted musicians to take up the instrument; as a result, the guitar was placed firmly on the concert platform.

27.1 **The famous 'papier mâché' guitar**

28   IGNACIO FLETA AND HIS SONS

When I entered the Fletas' studio, I was immediately struck by the lack of space, but everything was there— the benches, moulds, tools, wood stacked against the walls and on shelves, and guitars in all stages of construction. Not a square centimetre had been wasted. The famous and exceptionally beautiful Fleta guitars have always been made in these two, tiny, inter-connecting workshops on the first floor of a tall building in the old part of Barcelona. Ignacio Fleta started his career in 1911, and since his death on 11th August 1977 at the age of 80, his two sons, Francisco and Gabriel, have continued the business. He was making cellos, violas, violins and so-called 'ancient' stringed instruments in those early years, and a glass-fronted cabinet contains some fine examples. His sons have vivid memories of playing together amongst the shavings when they were small children, while their father worked. As they grew up, he taught them the rudiments of instrument making, and Gabriel told me that he made a little violin when he was still a boy.

28.1 **Ignacio Fleta, 1972**

28.2 **Francisco and Gabriel Fleta**

Their father started making guitars in 1928–30, but during and after the war, materials of the quality he demanded were difficult to obtain; he occasionally used maple for the backs and sides, and some woods from Africa. Even today, all their wood has to be imported, mostly from Germany, but some species come from America. It wasn't until about 1950, when Andrés Segovia started to use a Fleta for some of his concert performances, that Ignacio's guitar-making business really began to flourish. His instruments have since become the most sought-after in the world, being renowned for their quality of tone, combined with perfect style and workmanship. Many of the greatest guitarists of our age have owned Fleta guitars, and signed photographs of these artists, with their written tributes, adorn the walls of the studio.

Although the brothers are continuing to use materials, tools and moulds left to them by their father, they are individualists like all artist-craftsmen, and have their own ideas about how a top quality guitar should be put together. All operations are performed by hand, using the same tools that were used 100 to 200 years ago, at a production rate of fifteen guitars a year. I visited them in April 1980, and I was impressed by the enthusiasm and love for their craft which shone in both their faces. Although quite different in character, they obviously work together extremely well. We talked for two hours, with the assistance of an interpreter, and they were very kind and generous in answering my questions.

They demonstrated their side-bending technique on their father's old electrically heated bending iron, a vertical steel pipe about 10cm in diameter, and 60cm high, with a heating element inside (28.3). The rosewood sides (they use both Brazilian and Indian) are dampened during the bending process, and fitted round an inside mould. They are then glued to a large top-block which is held in a notch in the mould. The lower end of the body is dealt with in the same way, but using a much smaller block.

I was surprised to hear that they have started to use modern, synthetic glue for every operation. I was shown a pot of it—a thick, white emulsion that we call 'white glue', or P.V.A. They are very satisfied with it, and say that it is better than animal glue in every way—structurally and harmonically—and also that it is better for gluing rosewood than the traditional glue. Some types of white glue, they said, are unsatisfactory, because they 'dry spongy', but the best kind dries hard and transparent. When I mentioned the old objection to these glues—that you can't separate a joint with hot water and a knife—they explained that it can be done with alcohol and a thin spatula. Next come the linings. They prefer kerfed linings, top and bottom, and think that the method of gluing in little blocks, or 'tentel-lones', is not as strong, 'because some places are left unsupported'. They clamp the linings to the sides with outsized clothes-pegs in the usual manner.

The sound-board of a Fleta, as you can imagine, is quite literally, a work of art. Time and expense is not spared in the selection of either the finest quality, radially-sawn spruce (*Picea excelsa*), or cedar from Canada. The wood has been well seasoned before being stored in the workshop for a further two years, and I was shown several stacks of these boards, with about ten to a stack, tied round with thick string with spacers in between. They told me that they put these

bundles outside the window in the sun during this period for the final 'curing' process before being planed and jointed.

Every sound-board is treated differently after the jointing operation, depending on the character of the wood. When I talked to Gabriel and Francisco about this aspect of guitar-making, I sensed in them an almost spiritual affinity with the material. They have obviously inherited this feeling from their father, who, they said, tried to put a 'soul' into his guitars as he had into his violins. They described it as, 'the feeling of the wood—what it has to be'. The thickness across the board varies in accordance with this intuitive feeling, and it ranges from a little under, to just over, 2mm. They use the old style caliper gauge (see Chapters 4 and 16), combined with the 'tapping and listening' method, to arrive at the desired sound.

The rosette design originated by their father is still in use, (28.4) and they make enough for five instruments at one time. They showed me the intricate little blocks of coloured veneer that are fitted exquisitely together to make up the distinctive rosette of a Fleta guitar. For

28.3 **Francisco bending a rosewood side**

28.4 **The Fleta rosette**

them, however, rosette making is the least enjoyable aspect of guitar construction, and they said that they put it off for as long as possible!

Before gluing the sound-board on to the sides and linings, the strutting system is completed. They find now that a nine fan-strut arrangement suits their sound-boards best, with two 'harmonic' bars below the sound-hole, the lower one being set diagonally. A wooden 'plate' is glued under the strutting below the bridge, or 'under the nerve', as they call it. 'The guitar stays in the mould till the last minute' said Gabriel. 'The sound-board is glued on, then we put the mould away, when the instrument is completely dry and stable'.

Next come the edgings and purflings, which are bent and built up in the usual way. They make up their own purfling strips by gluing together alternate layers of black, white and blue veneer, and then cutting the 'sandwich' into strips. It is not until this advanced stage has been reached that the Honduras cedar neck is fitted. A number of these previously assembled neck blanks can be seen hanging up in the workshop (28.3). The heads are complete with their facings, and have been drilled for the tuning machines. A flat outlet ramp for the strings is always used (see Chapter 10). The heels are carved from a solid block of cedar which has been glued to the neck blank.

The joint between neck and body is where Ignacio Fleta departed from the traditional Spanish method. He adopted, quite naturally, the dovetail joint which he used for his violins and cellos, and his sons see no reason to change. In fact, they assert that the end result is much stronger than with the traditional joint. It must take them a long time to make, though, because they told me that it is so close-fitting that glue is not really necessary. Nevertheless, they use some! After the ebony finger-board has been glued on, fretting is begun.

The scale-length they have always used is the Torres 65cm. Ignacio Fleta was a great admirer of Torres, and he was influenced by the old master to the extent that for a long time he used the Torres seven fan-strut system. He was also inspired by Torres when he designed the head shape. The brothers showed me the template, made from brass, for marking out the fret positions. It is shaped like the finger-board, with the fret spacings engraved on it. At the ends of each engraved line a small hole is drilled, through which the finger-board is marked with a steel point. The fretting on a Fleta guitar is of exceptional quality. Each fret is finished with infinite care, and I can remember my guitar teacher, Len Williams (father of the famous John), saying during a lesson in 1961, that the frets are so beautifully made that you could mount one on a piece of walnut and keep it on the mantelpiece as an ornament!

Gold-plated tuning machines purchased in Barcelona, are fitted and then removed, ready for the finishing process. After a thin film of French polish has been applied, the grain of the rosewood sides and back is filled with a mixture of fine pumice-powder and alcohol. When this has dried and been rubbed down, the long, slow process of French polishing is begun. This is an art in itself, and when performed with the skill of the Fleta brothers, a remarkable effect is achieved. The fine woods acquire a deep, glowing colour, with a surface like glass. The bridge is not glued on until varnishing is nearly finished, the area of the sound-board that the bridge will occupy having been masked off with glued paper. Then, with the bridge finally in position, the strings are tied on and the 'action' adjusted before the last treatment with French polish to bring the surface finish to perfection.

They always make the same size and shape of guitar, but the interior is changing over the years. 'We put in new things—little modifications' said Gabriel, 'our harmonic bars are getting better—producing a warmer sound, but it's a very gradual process'.

When I asked them which part of the construction they considered to be the most important for tone quality, Francisco replied, 'The sound-board, but it's really the balance of everything—you have to find the right balance. Everything is important, but it's the thickness of the wood—any variation is important—it's impossible to be specific about it. Each guitar is telling us what to do!'

I finally left Barcelona knowing that I had witnessed artistry and craftsmanship that cannot be bettered anywhere in the world.

29 ROBERT BOUCHET

ROBERT BOUCHET, luthier, artist, and master crafts-man, is one of those rare beings who has succeeded in combining freedom of expression with a meticulous approach to detail. He is a man of many talents, and over the years, has produced a succession of exquisite model ships, carved his own frames for his paintings, and played the violin.

When I met him for the first time in Paris in 1979, I felt immediately that here was a happy man who had retained a boyish attitude to life in spite of his 82 years. His twinkling eyes greeted me with warmth and enthusiasm, and I knew from the first moment that we were going to be friends. Almost immediately we were launched into his favourite subject (and mine), guitar making; fortunately, his English is very good so communication was no problem. Towards the end of our session, lasting over four hours, I expressed concern about over-tiring him, but this was brushed aside with an infectious laugh, and later, his wife told me that he never tires of talking about guitars and demonstrating his method of making them.

In his small studio flat in Montmartre (where he also paints in the impressionist style), he led me up a short flight of carpeted stairs to his work-shop, and it was like entering Paradise! I was immediately struck by his tidiness. Every one of his hundreds of tools and implements has its own special shelf or hook, so that, in spite of the small size of the room, there was no sense of over-crowding. He showed me his beautifully con-structed jigs and clamps. Like all the best craftsmen, he has found it necessary to make most of his own tools, and he has built up a unique collection. They are highly individualised, and in many cases, extremely com-plicated; a clamping device for the fan-strutting for instance, made from aluminium strips and mahogany; the bridge clamping jig shown in *29.1*; and an ingenious gadget for thinning strips of veneer down by as little as one tenth of a millimetre. It is shown in *29.2*, and he demonstrated it for me with a long strip of rosewood.

The material is pulled through the gap under the cutter in the traditional manner, but the finely adjustable, sloping block of aluminium (worked with the little crank handle at the top), combined with the angled blade, provides an infinite range of thicknesses.

Monsieur Bouchet has been making guitars for 35 years, and his first instrument is still in his possession. He made the sound-board, he told me, by removing a plank from his cupboard, sawing it edgewise by hand before jointing it in the usual way to provide the symmetrical halves. The grain, as you can imagine, is a little on the coarse side! He calls it 'a very funny thing', but I tried it for tone, and it has a remarkable sonority.

29.1 **A bridge clamping device**
29.2 **Veneer strip thinning tool**

He is a great admirer of Torres, and based the design of his first guitars on the master's instruments. He studied and experimented alone, as well as making many visits to the studio of the renowned luthier, Ramirez, who, fortunately for Monsieur Bouchet, was working in Paris at the time. The hard work continued after the war, his instruments inevitably improved, and he gradually became known as a luthier of some significance. He was still basing his design on Torres, however, and it wasn't until 1957 that he made a major breakthrough. This came about when he realised that even the Grand Old Master's work could be improved upon! He became more and more convinced that the design of the sound-board was of prime importance in tone production, the strutting in particular. He was aiming for that elusive evenness of sound over the whole compass of the guitar. By slow, painstaking work, he evolved a system of strutting which included a bar of specific dimensions beneath the bridge. This arrangement, with its seven fan-struts and no V'ed struts at the base, he believes, comes very close to perfection. The grain of the struts runs in planned directions to give more or less flexibility in certain areas of the sound-board.

He was a drawing master then at the School of Decorative Art, making his guitars in his spare time, and there was in Paris, a classical guitar society called 'Les Amis de la Guitare' where some of the prominent

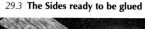
29.3 **The Sides ready to be glued**

players of that period used to meet every Friday to perform and discuss their problems. Monsieur Bouchet took one of his guitars along one day where it was greatly admired, and he began to receive the first orders for his instruments. Since then, some of the world's leading classical guitarists have owned and performed on Bouchet guitars, and he told me that he has more orders now than he can cope with before moving on to the next world!

He demonstrated his technique for me. Working in the traditional way, using the Spanish method of construction (29.3) he makes everything himself: rosettes, purfling strips and edgings; he even engraves and carves the tuning-machine plates and buttons. He designed, engraved and made the prints for his own distinctive label. Moulds were dispensed with a long time ago but he recommends the use of one for a beginner. He bends his sides dry on a gas-fired metal pipe, oval in section. He damps the area of the waist, but is very much opposed to soaking or boiling the wood. He glues paper on the outside of his sides for reinforcement and protection whilst working. The cedar neck, head, heel and foot, are first glued down on to the already strutted sound-board (he uses only animal glue) and the bent rosewood sides are then laid on top with the ends let into the heel slots. A collection of specially angled blocks (called 'tentellones' by the Spaniards), are then glued in the angle between sound-board and sides in a continuous line, without gaps. Next, he fits a kerfed lining for the back, and then he glues the strutted rosewood back itself, tying it down in the usual way. Every operation is made easier by his ingenious array of carefully conceived implements. When the purfling and fretting is complete, the bridge is glued on, and he gives the sound-board a coat of size made of very thin glue, rubbed on with cotton-wool.

His production is now down to about one guitar a year, and I tried out one of his latest guitars in his studio. As well as being a thing of beauty, it had a strong, resonating bass combined with a bell-like penetration in the treble. His instruments have been described as possessing a unique Debussy sound, very French like their gifted maker; and to finish them—French polish. He makes it himself!

30 JOSÉ ROMANILLOS

José Romanillos, now a luthier with an international reputation, was born in Spain but works in England. His guitars are played by top recitalists all over the world, including Julian Bream, Sergio Abreu, Charles Ramirez and Anthea Gifford; many others are on the long waiting list. He is a man gifted with all the necessary attributes: master craftsmanship, dedication, a deep appreciation of the finer aspects of instrument making, and an enquiring mind.

Our conversation took place in his hilltop bungalow situated in a remote corner of Wiltshire, and he was happy for me to use my tape recorder. His workshop is the nerve-centre of the house, and he produces on average fourteen guitars a year, plus an occasional lute and vihuela (an ancestor of the guitar). This amount of work entails long hours at his bench every day, and he told me that his English wife relieves him of most of the adminstrative pressures. For relaxation he plays cricket with Julian Bream, and also in the local team.

DOUBTFIRE. Where do you go for your materials?

ROMANILLOS. I get nearly all of it from abroad. The sound-boards I get from Switzerland. I buy the trees and cut them to my requirements—it's the ordinary Christmas tree, *Picea excelsa*. There's a great tradition that goes back to Greek times. They say that the trees should be cut at a certain time—on the waning moon. If you don't cut them at the right time they're more open to the attack of fungi.

DOUBTFIRE. Unless you are actually on the spot and can say, 'I want that tree,' it must be difficult.

ROMANILLOS. I have done that—walked around the forest and picked the trees. One goes by how round the trunk is, and how straight—it mustn't have any spiral growth.

DOUBTFIRE. What diameter would they be?

ROMANILLOS. The mean diameter would be about 55cm. They take over 200 years to grow.

DOUBTFIRE. I see you use rosewood for your backs and sides.

ROMANILLOS. Yes. It comes from India or Brazil. The Brazilian species is running out and you can't get good enough timber to make guitars. The one from India is mostly used these days because you get a better cut. This is what I use for the back and sides—it's all quarter-sawn. The neck is made out of Brazilian or Honduras cedar. Some English makers use mahogany—the African variety—but the Spaniards use cedar. There is a booklet that gives all the addresses of the importers—everything from polish to ivory. (*See Chapter 2: List of Suppliers*).

DOUBTFIRE. When you bend your sides, do you do this wet or dry?

ROMANILLOS. It varies. I tend to do them dry, but you've got to be very careful. I think it's advisable to soak them for a while—put them in water for about an hour—but I've done it all ways.

DOUBTFIRE. Do you think it has any noticeable effect on the tone of the instrument—the way you bend the sides?

ROMANILLOS. No, I don't think so. I have soaked the sides in a mixture of methylated spirits and water for a long time and then put them on formers and kept them for many days until they retain the form. Perhaps that's the best way to do it because the fibres of the wood don't get strained so much. When you bend them with heat the fibres must go through a tremendous stress, and that probably takes a little bit of elasticity out of the

30.2 **At work on a vihuela Sound-board**

sides. I can't say that I have noticed any difference at all in the sound. The traditional way is to soak it and heat it on a hot pipe. At the waist, where you have to apply most heat, I have two pieces of veneer soaked in water, and I put them between the bending iron and the side.

DOUBTFIRE. And then do you fit everything into a mould?

ROMANILLOS. No. I work in the Spanish method which is free. I have the sound-board on a work form, and I already have the outline of the guitar, and I bring my sides to it, and I clamp them around. Then I glue blocks inside.

DOUBTFIRE. This is a method for the expert. Don't you think it would be advisable for a beginner to use a mould?

ROMANILLOS. I would recommend that, yes, unless he's already a skilled wood-worker. Eventually though, he might want to experiment with sizes, and if he's going to make a mould for every one, he'll clutter up his workshop with eight or ten different moulds, so finally I think it's better to work freely.

DOUBTFIRE. What system of strutting do you use under the sound-board?

ROMANILLOS. The strutting has so many variations— the guitar-maker who finds the system that works for him—that's the right system!

DOUBTFIRE. But not to stick too rigidly I suppose?

ROMANILLOS. Well, you have to start from some-where. Probably the Torres pattern is basically right. Before he arrived, the central Europeans had another system which was more or less based on the lute, with transverse bars going across. That system is finished— nobody uses that for the classical guitar. The basic principle of strutting is to give strength to the sound-board—to hold the top, yet with enough resilience so that you can reduce the thickness. You can get strength by putting on a thicker top—that's what they used to do—no struts, thicker top. In order to thin the top you have to add strength, you have to support it. The struts play another role—particularly the fan struts—sound travels faster along the grain than across it, so in a way they help to spread it. But for me, the basic principle is to give strength to the guitar. I'm sure that if you could make a very thin top without strutting, it would probably sound better but it's not possible for structural reasons.

DOUBTFIRE. Do you vary your strutting system?

ROMANILLOS. I do—I tend to mess about with it

sometimes. Obviously it's always on the same theme, as it were, at least it's not far from it.

DOUBTFIRE. Have you ever completely originated your own system?

ROMANILLOS. Yes, early in my career I have made a few queer things. Recently, in the States, they've been trying to make a scientific guitar using modern technology.

DOUBTFIRE. How's this working out?

ROMANILLOS. Apparently, not very well. They sound loud, but they haven't got the quality. What I think they tend to forget is that scientific sense might not be acoustic sense, or guitar sense. In fact, I might say that

they don't have all the deficiencies the human guitar-maker gets in his instrument, and that's what gives the quality—those deficiencies. The point is, you have a tuning fork—purest sound—and it gets very boring after a time. I'm very interested in all this experimentation of course, but I think, ultimately, you have to have a human quality—it's difficult to define.

DOUBTFIRE. You could almost say a spiritual quality?

ROMANILLOS. Well, it is. The analysts will probably say it's nonsense, but the proof of the pudding is that every guitar-maker produces a different sound—different subtleties. Your hand-writing is different from mine.

DOUBTFIRE. I believe you use a bridge-bar under the sound-board, which Torres didn't do. Do you think this gives more balance from bass to treble?

ROMANILLOS. Well, it is a help. The counter agent, as it were, inside, helps to distribute the tension—to pull the whole top at the same time. Now, whether that evens the strings out, I wouldn't know. In order to prove a theory you have to do it under controlled laboratory experiments and this can't easily be done, so therefore you are influenced by what you hear or what you feel, or how you get up in the morning!

DOUBTFIRE. What do you consider to be the most important aspect in the construction of a sound-board with regard to tone production?

ROMANILLOS. I would say thickness, though obviously, the strutting plays a role in it. But it's the

117

thicknesses and the material you use that's most important.

DOUBTFIRE. Do you vary the thickness then, across the sound-board?

ROMANILLOS. I do—I'll do all sorts of things. I can't say specifically, I do this or that, you vary according to what you think is right, from 3mm to 2½ to 1½, and you have to assess the possibilities of that sound-board. There's no other way to do it—the density of the wood varies even from the same tree in accordance with how it's cut.

DOUBTFIRE. This is the beauty, of course.

ROMANILLOS. The whole thing, yes—and the whole, frustrating thing as well, sometimes!

DOUBTFIRE. This thickness that we talked about—do you measure it?

ROMANILLOS. I do. I have a caliper, but more than that—once the guitar is together, I get a bridge and flex the sound-board to see how it feels.

DOUBTFIRE. Do you think a larger body produces more tone?

ROMANILLOS. Not necessarily. It's a natural tendency when you see a big guitar to say that it sounds better, but if the sound is out of focus the body makes no difference.

DOUBTFIRE. When you say, 'the sound is out of focus', what exactly do you mean?

ROMANILLOS. You notice it when they play Bach—you have all the voices—you don't hear the sounds clearly, they're intermingled. This is because the body of the guitar is not working, it's not reproducing the notes singly as it should.

DOUBTFIRE. Yes, it's wonderful when you hear Bream play, for instance, it sounds like three guitars!

ROMANILLOS. This is it. A lot of these big-bodied guitars haven't got it because they're out of focus in that sense—it's the string working rather than the sound-board. I'm concerned now with making a very light guitar, yet strong—it's personal, subjective. They're more difficult to build because they're always borderline, you know, right on the edge. They are more responsive, but it takes a good player to know how to get the range out of them. To build a heavy guitar is easy—you know more or less what you're going to get. In a light guitar you get a lot of overtones going on, but if you can control them the sound is richer. On the

heavily-built guitar, because the timber is thicker you've got more stresses, the tensions are greater. If you get a guitar which is properly balanced, the tension on the sound-board is minimal—it's pure resonance.

DOUBTFIRE. Would you call guitar-making an art rather than a craft?

ROMANILLOS. It's not recognised as such. They still call us craftsmen or artisans, but it really *is* an art because you've got to create all the time. They call a carver an artist. A guitar-maker hasn't only got to carve, as it were, but he has to produce sound, which is very elusive. You've got your own experience that tells you—if you do this you're going to get that—but it's one of those crafts, or arts, where you're always in the dark somehow. I'm talking on a very high level, of course, about producing the ultimate.

DOUBTFIRE. You must have come very close to it sometimes.

ROMANILLOS. Well, I have made some guitars that have given me a great sense of achievement, and it's very gratifying to know that people are enjoying them.

DOUBTFIRE. It must have given you a great thrill when you heard one of your guitars being played by Julian Bream for the first time.

ROMANILLOS. It was fantastic! When I first started, it was the ultimate for me—I'd dreamt of that chap playing my guitars and it was like a dream come true. In fact it was at the Aldeburgh Festival, and that day I met Benjamin Britten and Peter Pears. It was really great, but now, that dream gone, all I'm interested in is how to produce a better guitar.

DOUBTFIRE. What started you off on your guitar making career?

ROMANILLOS. The whole thing began when I made my first instrument on the kitchen table. I couldn't understand that by putting a few pieces of wood together you could make some sound—this in itself was a mystery to me, and I've had the feeling ever since. It excited me, and it gave me the desire to understand something about it—the opportunity and incentive to be always working for something unknown. To me it has a tremendous meaning. Trying to understand such a problem, that's what fascinates me—the practical thing. I see an horizon which is always there, you know, but one never gets to it. You do other jobs and they're limited, but this—it's bottomless—the possibilities are tremendous, there's always a sense of excitement about producing the ultimate, and I'm conceited enough to think that one day I'll do it!

INDEX

Figures in bold type indicate illustrations